ILLUSTRATED GUIDE TO COLLECTING
ANTIQUES

ILLUSTRATED GUIDE TO COLLECTING
ANTIQUES

RONALD PEARSALL

TODTRI

This book was designed and produced by Todtri Productions Limited
P.O. Box 572, New York, NY 10116-0572 FAX: (212) 695-6984

Printed and bound in Singapore

ISBN 1-57717-000-8

Author: Ronald Pearsall

Publisher: Robert M. Tod
Designer and Art Director: Ron Pickless
Editor: Nicolas Wright
Typeset and DTP: Blanc Verso/UK

Contents

Introduction

I t is a truism that you only get what you pay for. But not in antiques. There are few fields in which it is possible to buy something for a few dollars or pounds (or francs or roubles) and subsequently to sell the same item for a thousand times as much. It is also a truism that all antiques increase in real value. They do not. Silver has never really recovered from the sad day in the 1970s when the bottom dropped out of the market, and oak furniture made before the eighteenth century has steadily dropped in value in real terms over the last twenty-five years.

This gives an edge to any collector with an eye. Will he or she spot

something that will rocket in value? Original Walt Disney cartoon cels? 78 rpm discs of the classic greats of rock 'n' roll? Or will the collector latch on to something whose time has come and gone and be left with what in the antique trade is known as "a dog"?

Not all collectors are out to make money, of course. If they want a particular object to live with, they buy it – if they can afford it. Some pieces are out of reach for all but museums and the very wealthiest of people, but there are a thousand times more articles out there on the streets, waiting to be spotted and sometimes not recognized for what they are.

Collecting can open a window on the past. There will be surprises, revelations and culture shocks. And it can cost next to nothing. The collector has to be shrewd and to be aware that anything that is half-way decent has been and is being forged and faked. One in five pictures (some say one in four) that passes through a sale-room is a fake or at least not what it pretends to be. The aim of the collector is to avoid the fake or to find something that no one else has started to fake.

What are antiques? Should they be called collectables? This book will cover the entire range – furniture, pottery and porcelain, domestic antiques, the fast-growing field of industrial and office antiques, silver, clocks and watches, glass, pictures and prints, ephemera – in short, the whole range of objects of days gone by. Some would say that some of these are not antiques – but they are.

An Affordable Start

Antiques of whatever kind, from a humble postcard from a seaside town to a wardrobe 8 feet (2.4 metres) wide, are a window on the past. They make history come alive. They have an aura, and it is small wonder that millions of people become fascinated by them, even if they only ever see them in television programmes about antiques.

There are those antiques that are out of the reach of all except museums and the super-rich, but there are also items from the same period, even pieces that look nearly the same, that are within the grasp of almost anybody. There are those antiques that the reader will be able to admire only from a distance, but there are parallels in other fields. For every one who can afford a Ferrari, for example, there are a thousand who can manage to buy a Ford. But it does not matter if an object that is beautiful or interesting or is in some way typical of its time is valued at £20 or $20 or £20,000 or $20,000 – it still has an aura of something intangible.

What is meant by affordable? This is an impossible question, for it will vary from person to person. For practical purposes, however, a top figure of £500 ($775) has been adopted, especially for furniture. However, some of the antiques mentioned will be only £5 ($7.75) and some may be even less.

The classic antique - a George III mahogany chair of about 1790, with its own unique style, such as the large seat. A set of four would be immensely expensive, but not so a single.

FURNITURE

Furniture was the basis of the antique trade, and it is still by far the most important category. English furniture shows parallels with that made on the continent of Europe, which was, until about 1660, rather more advanced. Early existing furniture is of oak. Little furniture from before 1500 survives, however, but sixteenth and seventeenth-century furniture is relatively common, and can be bought because it is resolutely out of fashion. Sometimes it is as cheap now as it was twenty years ago, even allowing for high rates of inflation. Stools, chests and small tables can be regarded as decidedly affordable.

Walnut and lacquered furniture followed oak in about 1660, although oak was still used, especially in country areas, and furniture made with the new materials is far more expensive. In the eighteenth century mahogany began to be used. Lesser examples can be bought reasonably, and much furniture of the succeeding periods is in the "affordable" price bracket. An important exception is Regency furniture. The historical Regency lasted from 1811 to 1820, but the term is often used loosely for a much longer time span, a period in which rosewood featured prominently. Edwardian mahogany has been appreciating in value for some years after a period of total neglect. Arts and Crafts furniture, made between about 1880 and 1910, can look surprisingly modern. The makers often used stained oak with pewter and other unusual fittings, and its value depends much on the maker. It is often of superb quality, and should be bought.

All early American furniture is rare and expensive, and eighteenth-century mahogany furniture is the equal of that of the great British cabinet-makers. Nineteenth-century American furniture (the equivalent of the British Victorian period) was made in immense quantities and is buyable. America was in the forefront of the Art Deco movement, but furniture of the 1920s and 1930s may not be recognized as such. If you see examples from this period, acquire them if possible because items in this style are enjoying an upsurge in popularity.

Unusual and curious furniture is emerging from eastern Europe at present, and it is sometimes difficult to categorize. In the eighteenth century most European countries copied or assimilated English mahogany styles, but each nation had its own individual stylistic flourishes. Russian furniture was especially innovative and incorporated imaginative variations on French and English models.

Furniture from the Far East did not go through the plethora of fashions, and it is, therefore, difficult to date by most collectors. It is a fairly specialized field, and could be a trap for the unwary.

CERAMICS

When it comes to pottery and porcelain, values depend less on the object than on its date and the factory that made it. Porcelain and pottery are both made from clay, but pottery is fired at a lower temperature. Hard-paste porcelain was first made in the West in 1709 in imitation of pieces made by the Chinese, who had invented the process more than a thousand years earlier. Pottery has been made from primitive times because it needs a quite modest temperature, but pottery is not necessarily of an inferior status. Except for the presti-

gious factories such as Bow – always unmarked for those who want to buy the unattainable! – or Chelsea, much classic porcelain is available at affordable prices. Worcester, which began production in 1751, was a very prolific factory, and although pieces are by and large expensive, they are worth looking out for because so much was made and exported.

Blue-and-white items of china and pottery are among the most desirable of antiques, especially when transfer-printed with scenes. Blue was widely used because cobalt colouring was technically the most suitable for decorating the ceramic surface. A collection of old blue-and-white pieces makes a superb display, and it is affordable, even cheap, although do not be deceived by relatively modern ware. If the mark includes the words "Made in England" it will be later than 1890.

Huge amounts of porcelain and pottery were produced in the nineteenth century, some good, some bad, and much indifferent. The last kind can be picked up for very little, but it should be avoided because it is often not even worth what you will pay for it. More modern ware fluctuates with fashion, and to buy on a name alone is hazardous.

Studio pottery, which was often underwritten by the major factories such as Minton, and art pottery form a fascinating and choice area, because only the major names fetch big money. The work of unknown art potters can be equally good. It is often very simple and devoid of ornament – the shape and proportions are the criteria by which it is judged. When such items are unmarked, they enter the domain of the "expert", so beware.

Clarice Cliff, who designed boldly patterned wares in the 1920s and 1930s, has peaked and prices have begun to adjust themselves. Charlotte Rhead is regarded by many as a far superior potter, but collectors have never come to terms with her works. Susie Cooper is the third "name" of the interwar years, but there were hundreds of fine potteries, some of which are ill-researched, producing interesting and vastly underrated pieces. Two art potters that are worth looking out for are Pilkington and Ruskin, whose output, at present getting fair prices, is somewhat neglected. Factories that are currently very much in favour, such as Shelley (1872–1966), produced some very mundane pieces. Among other 1930s ceramics that are beginning to appear on the market, Sylvac represents what may, perhaps, be called the bargain basement, with the "motto ware" made in Torquay, Devon, running it close.

Buy pieces for their quality, their distinction, even their novelty value. Do not buy on the strength of the name on the base. If you become especially interested in the work of a single maker or factory, consider joining one of the specialist collectors' clubs, which often organize lectures and tours, and which will give you the opportunity to meet like-minded enthusiasts. Many such societies also produce their own newsletters.

GLASS

Glass is easy to make: the basic ingredient is sand, so we have glass from every period, including Roman. Despite its fragility, it is possible to build up a representative collection of glass for very little out-

Opposite: A pair of fine Irish Waterford cut-glass decanters, both decorative and useful, though decanters have never been collected with the enthusiasm that surrounds drinking glasses.

lay, although genuine Venetian glass will be beyond the means of all but the richest collectors. There is, however, an immense variety in wine glasses alone, with dozens of variations in the stem and the bowl. English glass that is not cloudy or inferior dates from 1674, when lead was introduced into the mix. Cutting became less delicate in the nineteenth century, leading to "prickly monstrosities", with diamond-shaped cutting in high relief that looks very elaborate and spectacular, and decanters followed the same path – from the simple to the over-elaborate.

Colour could be easily introduced into the glass mix, and the glass produced by French makers such as Emile Gallé and Americans such as Louis Comfort Tiffany is superb – and expensive. Equally collectable and attractive, in its more modest way, is some of the commercial coloured glass of the 1920s and 1930s, which is still available for next to nothing.

So, too, with bottles – poison bottles, beer bottles, scent bottles and so forth are all worth collecting, and there is a vast range available. Paperweights have long been collected, and although the classic

Opposite: A Clarice Cliff bowl from the interwar years, once no more than chain-store merchandise retailed at a few cents, pennies, centimes or pfennigs.

This might well seem to be American Tiffany glass worth four figures. It is, in fact, a high-quality replica within the pocket of almost anybody.

French factories of St Louis, Baccarat and Clichy made paperweights of great value, humbler examples are readily available, and an interesting collection can be made of oddities at little cost.

METALWORK AND JEWELLERY

It has been estimated that fewer than four hundred English-made silver articles survive from the period prior to 1525. Until the nineteenth century silver was cheap, and items made from it were not highly regarded and were often melted down to make something else. It is still not expensive and is easily recognized. British silver has a unique identification system of hallmarks (handbooks on which are plentiful), and is, for that reason, particularly collectable. However, European and American silver is also available, and this is an open field to anyone with limited buying power. Do not be deceived by marks intended to confuse, which at first glance look convincing. Memorize the "look" of genuine marks, not the actual date letters. Large items of silver, even the ugly and malformed, are horrendously expensive.

The first substitute for silver was Sheffield plate, which was discovered in 1743. Silver plate is a thin layer of silver over a base metal, first applied by hand, later by electrolysis. Some examples, such as that by the firm of Elkington, are highly collectable, but many are not. Silver plate in middle of the range ages badly – the silver wears off, exposing the base metal.

Pewter was the poor man's silver, and some pieces bear fake marks, intended to deceive, for when it is highly polished pewter can look like silver at first glance. Early British pewter is expensive, but later pieces, which have the initials of the monarch impressed into the metal (verification marks) and which enjoyed a revival at the turn of this century, are not expensive. It is a very agreeable alloy (of tin with varying amounts of copper, bismuth and sometimes lead) with a low melting point, and it was used for many utilitarian and decorative purposes. Even teaspoons were made of pewter – they tended to melt in the tea. Pewter mugs, which are still preferred by older beer drinkers, are quite cheap, and some examples have glass bottoms. Beware of Britannia metal (tin, antimony and copper), which is often mistaken for pewter but is less desirable and ages badly, although it, too, has its collectors.

Jewellery is a vast subject, and a favourite of dealers who want to keep all their stock in a suitcase. No one without a feel for jewellery should speculate, because cut glass can easily be confused with diamonds, natural pearls with cultured pearls, and coloured glass with gemstones. In no other field is it so important to get to know the genuine article. Gemstones can be put in new settings, the settings themselves can be cannibalized or cut down, and fake quality stones can be set in good high-carat gold settings. Nevertheless, this is a very rewarding area for those who have an instinct for the real thing.

CLOCKS AND WATCHES

It is not surprising that there are so many clock collectors, for there is something infinitely appealing about the tick-tick-tick of a small timepiece or the steady pulse of a longcase clock. It is advisable for collec-

tors to have a basic knowledge of clock mechanisms, so that, before buying, they can open up a clock and see if the movement looks "right" and has not been transplanted from another case. In some old clocks, movements have been upgraded without intent to deceive.

Interest among new collectors has shifted to twentieth-century clocks, which are still available at reasonable prices. These can be Art Deco clocks in a "sunburst" surround, oak mantel clocks with chimes or novelties. The most common "antique" clock is the Victorian "black marble" clock, which is, depressingly, actually of slate, not marble. A promising field is the twentieth-century alarm clock, of which there are hundreds, perhaps thousands, of varieties, often ingenious and appealing. Longcase clocks of a basic kind are available at affordable prices, but these are largely country clocks in oak and are not very thrilling. A practical point, of course, is that longcase clocks need space – if you live in a low-ceilinged house, this is not a field for you.

Millions of American clocks were sold in kit form by mail order for home assembly. The industry started as early as 1807, and it competed with clocks made in the Black Forest area of Germany, where the components were made from wood. These clocks could gain or lose twenty minutes a day. However, they led to the cuckoo clock, put in classic form about 1870. Carriage clocks have great appeal, but are expensive if they are of good quality. Modern

Above: A Victorian "marble" mantel clock made of slate. As recently as twenty-five years ago these were smashed up to get at the very good movement, and the case thrown away.

Opposite: A fine collection of carriage clocks, once intended to be carried in a leather box. The enamelled miniature clock at the foot of the photograph would be very desirable (this is true of most miniatures) if genuine.

Below: An Art Deco clock in a metal sur-round, unusual for the stylised monkeys. A square dial was then considered innovative.

Opposite: The French clock- and watch-maker Abraham Louis Breguet (1747-1823) is perhaps the most prestigious of all time. His designs are refined and simple, and he was the supreme master of clockwork. He is credited with the invention of the self-wind-ing watch.

carriage clocks may at first glance be taken for older ones, as the basic design has not altered.

Early watches are prohibitively expensive. The first to be made were spherical, then oval ones began to be made before they finally assumed their present form. Over the centuries, the watch was tech-nology at its peak – a masterpiece of compression. Musical move-ments were added, and played a tune when the watch chimed. The love affair with watches has continued, and modern Rolex watches are now in great demand. The Rolex name dates from 1925. Commercial pocket watches, with or without a hinged lid, unless of gold, are less desirable, for silver pocket watches were made by the million in the US, especially by the Waterbury Company from 1880, and in Britain, and they have little value. Wrist-watches, known as wristlets, were introduced in the 1880s, and were not worn by men until World War I when they were invaluable to soldiers in the trenches. Novelty watches of the 1920s and 1930s offer scope to collectors – the first alarm wrist-watch, the Cricket, was invented in 1947, for example, and would form the basis of a fascinating collection.

COINS AND MEDALS

Coins and medals form a collecting area subject to a good deal of misapprehension. Old coins, even Roman coins, are not necessarily rare. Most nineteenth-century copper coins from whatever country are worth little, although they are frequently splendidly made and would be a good and unusual starter collection. However, if they come from a particular year when few were minted, they can be valuable.

Certain coins are worth a great deal of money, although it is a shifting, mysterious subject to the outsider, and the collecting of coins is, perhaps, the most specialized field of all. In 1983 a £3 Charles I coin of 1643 was sold for £7500 ($11,625); in 1996 the same coin, after thirteen years of inflation, was sold for £5000 ($7750). Why? Was there something wrong with it? Was the price of 1983 a freak? Few can say with any certainty.

Rare coins, usually of gold, can lose their value very rapidly because so much bullion has been brought up, sometimes surreptitiously, from sunken vessels, especially Spanish galleons.

Bank notes is a fruitful collecting area. Notes should be in good

The collection of bonds, stocks, shares, and paper money, is a fairly recent development. Some collectors have found, by accident, that the shares they have bought for their collection are still valid, and valuable. It is a complicated area, akin to specialised stamp collecting, and the novice collector would be wise to do careful research beforehand.

condition. If they are uncirculated it is a plus, although pristine condition could, of course, mean that these may be suspect as possible fakes. If they are overprinted with the word "specimen" they are considerably more valuable. The billion mark notes from 1930s Germany are worth little.

There are two kinds of medals, military and commemorative. Until World War II medals bore the soldier's name, number, rank and unit. Soldiers and sailors who participated in various campaigns had bars added to their medals, and these bore details of the campaigns; these can be forged. Campaigns in which there were few participants naturally resulted in fewer bars, and these are the most sought after. Medals for heroism are far more valuable than those for long service or merely "being there". Standard-issue medals of World War I and World War II are of little value.

Commemorative medals range from prestigious sixteenth-century Italian and French medals to modest bronze medals for anything from agricultural shows to athletic events of this century. Often nicely made and usually boxed and mounted on velvet or silk, they would form a promising collection, and they are certainly inexpensive.

A very fine collection of medals including the prize of them all - the Victoria Cross, instituted in 1856 as a supreme award for gallantry in the Crimean War. The bars on the medals represent the campaigns the holder was involved in; in some campaigns, only a few soldiers took part. These bars are consequently rare - and faked.

A modest wooden coal scuttle, solid, useful, and unpretentious, usually made of oak. The carving on this example is better than some. Interesting and evocative household antiques can be acquired for very little outlay.

PERSONAL EFFECTS

Almost everything in the category of domestic antiques is affordable and collectable. The field of kitchen and cooking antiques alone is enormous, ranging as it does from standard fireside furniture – fenders, fire-irons, trivets, coal scuttles or bellows – to toasting forks, kettle-tilters (to protect the hands from burning) and pot-hooks (for keeping food warm but away from the flames of an open fire). The kitchen offers a multitude of collectables – copper kettles, jelly moulds, gingerbread moulds decorated with topical subjects (they can date back to Elizabethan times), specialized cooking equipment, such as broilers (frying-pans with two close-fitting pans hinged together), digesters (iron stock-pots with a valve to let the steam out), fish kettles, sugar boilers, and pestles and mortars. Mortars are often found without their pestles and used as garden ornaments. Chopping-boards and bread-boards were often attractively carved. In the grand houses even the simplest kitchen items would feature armorial crests. Especially attractive are coopered barrels – that is, barrels ringed with iron or brass bands. The coopering was not done for decorative reasons. It was to hold the staves in position when the wood became soaked through. Brass and copper articles, such as skimmers, warming-pans and similar kitchen equipment make fine displays, but

unfortunately, they are widely faked. Copper in particular is easily aged – look out for genuine signs of wear and loose rivets – and eschew miniatures, which are invariably tourist pieces.

Every kitchen was different. Sometimes there were facilities, even auxiliary rooms, for laundering, beer-brewing, bread-making and butchering. Flat-irons, evolved in the sixteenth century, have long been a cheap antique, sometimes painted and used as door-stops. Unfortunately they vary little, and to be interesting they should probably form part of a themed collection of kitchen bygones.

For collectors whose budget is limited, personal antiques provide variety and the joy of discovery at very little cost. They are also endlessly fascinating, revealing as they do facets of "real" life. Little in this area has been systematically categorized, and there are no comprehensive price guides and date lines as with, say, porcelain and silver. Collectors can choose, defining for themselves what a personal antique is and when it ceases to be a personal antique and becomes purely decorative, as in the case of some pieces of jewellery.

Personal antiques for men include shaving equipment. Until the 1880s the cut-throat razor was universal, but a break-through came in 1891 when the American Home Safety Razor was introduced. In 1903 William Gillette perfected the throw-away blade, and in 1931

There is a wide variety in kitchenalia, such as this nineteenth-century butter churn. More rarely, churns can be plain cylindrical objects with a pump action.

Opposite: A selection of shaving equipment on an art nouveau washstand (the tiles are unmistakeable). The convex shaving mirror on turned uprights is of exceptional quality, and the mother-of-pearl handled cut-throat razor is fairly uncommon.

the Schick Electric Razor was invented. Associated with razors are shaving-mugs, which are often ornate and were favourite souvenirs from the seaside. Shaving-stands were often very intricate and ingenious articles, with holders for everything, including toothbrushes, sometimes with silver handles. Men did not go in for cosmetics or deodorants, except for moustache and beard dye and the use of scented pomades and macassar oil for the hair. The electric toothbrush was invented about 1885, but was too far ahead of its time.

Until the Victorian period women had only a modest range of cosmetics, including powder and rouge. The earliest powders contained white lead and were poisonous, but the containers are very pretty and collectable. Later, face-powder was often made from rice powder in a restricted range of colours, but by 1925 Coty was producing nine different shades in twenty-one perfumes. Powder compacts would, on their own, form an interesting and decorative collection, and they range from prestige items made of gold and silver, with enamelled or inlaid decoration of mother-of-pearl, precious metals or gemstones, to early plastic examples.

All kinds of dressing-table memorabilia can be collected. Sets consisting of a matching brush, mirror and comb, and sometime clothes

Below: A range of 1920s and 1930s powder compacts, mostly enamelled, though silver and the new plastics were also used, often in combination.

Opposite: A richly encrusted bird of paradise brooch for evening wear, in which jewellery was flaunted. Daytime jewellery was more subdued and sedate.

Below: An enamelled box, perhaps Bilston, a generic name for enamels from the Birmingham area of England, which produced many more boxes than the more famous Battersea. Enamelled boxes, for pills, cosmetics, and other small objects, reached their peak in the eighteenth century.

brush, were popular, and they were often made with silver backs. These were sold very cheaply because the silver was wafer-thin and easily damaged. Tortoiseshell and ivory were also used in the days before plastic became ubiquitous. Ring stands were often made in the form of a human hand and from various materials. The variety of hat-pins is endless, and can form a charming collection on their own. Scent-bottles are a fascinating area. Some are double-ended, with one half designed to contain smelling salts (sal volatile). Many were made in coloured cut glass. Other antiques on the dressing table are enamelled boxes for pills, cosmetics, pins and odds and ends, and these can date back into the eighteenth century – look out especially for pieces from the great period of 1750 to 1780. Some boxes were made to hold patches or beauty spots that were stuck on the face to cover blemishes or draw attention to a fine feature. Glove-stretchers were essential when gloves were made of kid, and they come in many materials. By themselves, however, they can form a rather boring collection, because there is so little variety: that is why they are so cheap.

Fashions were reflected on the dressing table. Queen Victoria made all things Scottish popular, and items such as spectacle cases, work boxes and dressing cases were often decorated in tartan fabrics and ribbons.

Pin trays, which could be made from metal, wood, china, pottery or papier mâché, were often finely decorated, and pin cushions were made in all shapes – making them was a popular pastime for young ladies. One intriguing group are the heart-shaped, velvet-covered cushions, in which pins are pushed so that the heads form a message or a pattern.

As the railway network began to cover the country and better roads facilitated tourism, souvenirs proliferated, often bearing the name of a popular resort. These pieces are of variable quality but immensely interesting. They could include napkin rings, rulers, boxes of all shapes and sizes and made in all materials (including coal!), letter-openers, darning eggs, tape-measure holders – almost anything useful or useless might have the name of a resort emblazoned on it, and this is a field that offers almost unlimited and inexpensive opportunities for a new collector.

This is also true of collectables made from "substitute" materials, such as the synthetic resin Bakelite, which was discovered in 1909 and was much used for early radios, ash trays and so on. Other early synthetic materials include vulcanite, which was made from India-rubber and sulphur by means of a process discovered, accidentally,

A dressing table set, two brushes and a mirror. These could be in tortoiseshell or ivory, though ivorine, an early plastic, and imitation tortoiseshell were more often used, as well as silver.

by Charles Goodyear in 1839, and celluloid, which was widely used from the 1870s for dolls and toys but which was dangerously flammable and has not worn well. Many of these materials were not regarded as cheap alternatives, but as substances in their own right, and items made from these early plastic-like materials are now very collectable.

Writing antiques include pens (especially fountain pens), pencils, writing slopes and boxes, elaborate ink stands, ink-bottles (a popular collectable because there are hundreds of varieties) and pen-wipers (essential before the introduction of the fountain pen). With the introduction of the Penny Post in the Britain in 1840 and an increasingly literate population, thousands of letters were written daily. A collection based around the theme of writing could include old stationery, stamped envelopes and especially headed business stationery which frequently has fascinating pictorial vignettes.

Smoking-related antiques are a rich, if unfashionable, area. Until the middle of the nineteenth century, when cigarettes came into use, only cigars (dating from the mid-eighteenth century) and pipes were smoked. Early pipes were of clay, meerschaum (hydrated magnesium silicate) or porcelain, because no wood that would not catch fire was

A silver inkstand of unusual pattern, with a rack for various writing implements.

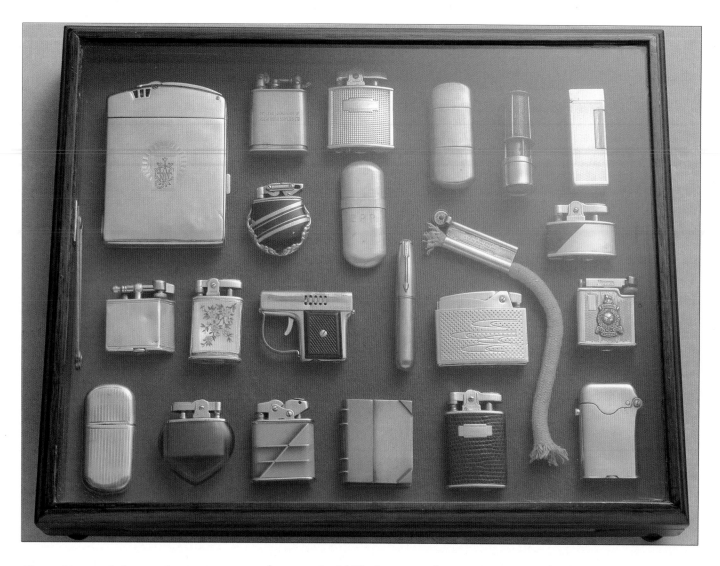

Above: Cigarette lighters and a cigarette case, ranging from the simple to the sophisticated, all working on the same principle of a flint struck against a cogwheel. Some early lighters, such as the Zippo, are now reproduced.

Opposite: A range of smoking implements and accessories. The cased pipe is of meerschaum with a mouthpiece of amber; these could be very expensive in their day, far more costly than they are today. Meerschaum was used because the flavour of the tobacco improved with age, and "well-smoked" meerschaums were greatly in demand.

known. In 1859 the root of an unpromising shrub was investigated, and the briar pipe was introduced. Tobacco was kept in often ornate jars or boxes, often lined with lead. To poke down the tobacco in the bowl of the pipe a wide variety of pipe-stoppers came into use, made of every conceivable substance. The first match was invented in 1827, called the Congreve, and although the technology improved, matches were still likely to burst into flames, so the air-tight vesta box was introduced. These were so popular that many fine small silver boxes were converted, including much more valuable snuff-boxes and vinaigrettes (tiny boxes containing sweet-smelling substances). Vesta boxes could be in almost any shape, including pigs and other animals, horseshoes, sentry boxes, bottles, boots, violins – anything, in fact, that would serve as a container.

Early petrol lighters were rather basic – cotton-wool, a flint, a wick and a cogged wheel, but in the 1920s they became decorative objects, often of great charm. Table-lighters were often disguised as something else – a cocktail bar or a golf ball. Lighter-watches by Dunhill are probably the most expensive accessory, worth in excess of £1,000 ($1,500).

Match holders were also popular, the basic shape being a flattened sphere, ribbed to provide a striking surface. Breweries found them an

ideal medium, second only to ash-trays, for displaying advertisements, and there is a wide range for an enterprising collecting, which is, considering the style and character often shown, very cheap. Throw-away items, such as match boxes, cigarette boxes and cigar boxes, have their collectors, too.

The most refined member of the tobacco family is snuff, which was taken from the seventeenth century, although nothing has survived from that time. In the eighteenth century snuff boxes were made of most materials, including gold, silver and brass. Until about 1740 the hinge stuck out at the back, but after that date it was set flush – a good dating tip, if a collector is lucky enough to come across an early specimen.

Clothing, of course, is intensely personal. Some old clothing is not what it appears to be – it can be fancy-dress costume or even theatrical costumes for operas and plays with a historical setting – and if the material is convincing it is sometimes difficult to differentiate. In modern times, collecting clothing bearing designer labels carries with

Opposite: Novelty lighters could be in any form or of almost any material, including silver, and were mainly table lighters. Some could be elaborately incorporated with pop-up cigarette holders, and as they were luxury items for the better off were usually of high quality.

Below: Snuff boxes and bottles, several of them oriental, where they were greatly prized, often made of jade, ivory, or fine porcelain. Snuff was widely used in the nineteenth century by all classes, but the use dropped off somewhat with the widespread introduction of cigarettes in the 1850s.

Opposite: The art on the leaves of fans could be magical, and the sticks could be intricately pierced until they seemed to be made of lace. The folding fan, often hand-painted by talented artists, is far more desirable than the fixed fan; it was used as an accessory for flirtation, and we see many references to it in this role in literature.

Below: Parasols were an essential accessory for women and girls when out of doors, and whereas men's umbrellas were dull and unimaginative - as there was still a lurking feeling that they were unmanly - the parasol could be a work of art. They are not so common as might be thought, as over the years they have deteriorated badly.

it the danger that the label is a fake or has been removed from the genuine article and inserted in a lesser make.

Clothing accessories include umbrellas, parasols and walking sticks. Novelty sticks have great variety. The best known is probably the sword stick, which was first used about 1780, but sticks can incorporate compasses, drink flasks, telescopes, watches, fishing tackle and even "detective" cameras. Some could be converted into ladders or artists' easels. Men's umbrellas have little variation, but parasols, which were first recorded in China in 1644 and became very popular in Europe towards the end of the nineteenth century and in the 1920s, come in a wide range of styles and colours. Many parasols were made of paper, so few survive in perfect condition. Even more vulnerable are fans, which were the essential accessory to an evening out. Many had superbly hand-painted decoration, often on paper or silk, with the sticks connected by ribbon. There are two types of fan, the rigid and the folding, and most collectors prefer the folding type. Even in a decayed state, fans are frequently minor works of art, yet damage reduces the value to almost nothing. For those who wish to possess beautiful objects, irrespective of condition, there is nothing more worthy than the fan in all its fragility.

Personal antiques is a very wide field, and of course can include possessions of the famous or infamous, or alleged personal possessions. A half-smoked cigar said to have been smoked by Sir Winston

Churchill is a non-starter. John Wayne's Stetson, on the other hand, was sold for £2580 ($4000), but it was fully authenticated.

Technological antiques is one of the fastest growing fields of collecting. This field encompasses scientific instruments, mechanical antiques such as sewing machines and typewriters, cameras and even clockwork toys, although rare examples by the top names can be hideously expensive. Old toys are a popular collecting area, and in this field, "old" may mean pieces that were made in the 1960s. Teddy bears, scale models, and Cindy and Barbie dolls all have their collectors.

There are thousands of different technological antiques, but there are certain common factors that make for collectability. The antique should be complete, in reasonable condition, rust-free and, if was originally supplied with accessories, they should accompany it. If it is in full working order, so much the better, although discretion must be used for rare prototypes. The more common the antique – such as a turn-of-the-century Remington typewriter or Kodak camera – the

Above: The Barlock typewriter of 1889, with its art nouveau design features, is perhaps the most handsome of all type-writers. Technically it was a dead end, for the hammers were "down hitting", so gravity did not bring them back.

Opposite: The sextant was introduced in the eighteenth century by Thomas Hadley in Britain and John Godfrey in the US, and in association with an accurate nautical clock (the chronometer) made navigation more certain. It was used to measure the angles of the stars and the sun. This is a lightweight model with struts instead of solid brass.

Opposite: Two wind-up gramophones and a horn gramophone, The wind-up gramophones had their speakers in the front, hidden by doors when not in use. Some gramophones had horns several feet long, and in the 1920s these were doubled back on themselves and concealed in a cabinet, which was often disguised as a piece of period furniture.

more perfect it needs to be. A microscope or a telescope can be tested on the spot; more elaborate instruments such as sextants need an understanding of how they work before you can check them.

As early high technology is more and more collected – wire recorders, tape recorders, pre-World War II televisions, valve radios, primitive laser machines and early computers – so more expertise is needed on the part of the buyer. And this is not the kind of information that is usually available to a general dealer. Some technology – that of the gramophone or phonograph – is simple, and if there is something wrong there are so few components that it is easy for a non-expert to locate the fault. If there is damage, it may cost a lot to put right – if the spring of a musical box or a gramophone, or even a clockwork toy, has broken, specialized help may be required. Small springs can be easily replaced, perhaps by cannibalizing something basically worthless; notched springs are usually fastened to a spur. A gramophone spring is powerful and dangerous – if it is "stuck", unwinding it can be hazardous, so seek expert help.

EPHEMERA

Ephemera are items that should have been thrown away, but somehow were not. They include bus, tram and train tickets, sporting programmes, theatre programmes, cinema and travel posters, election badges and stickers, bubble gum wraps and cards, packaging, film stills, comics, trade catalogues, cigarette cards and newspapers. Some ephemera, such as picture postcards, intended at first just to send a message, were collected almost from day one; others slide into collectability after decades. Victorian sheet music covers, especially of music-hall and, in America, vaudeville songs, have enjoyed a vogue since the 1960s but remain greatly under-priced. Recently, telephone cards enjoyed a vogue.

What becomes interesting is a matter of chance. Old photographs of churches are worthless; old photographs of street scenes or disasters can be valuable. Why are cigarette cartons of almost no concern, while matchbox labels have thousands of collectors and dozens of societies? The lesson would appear to be to throw away nothing and to save everything, but this is clearly impossible.

It is also difficult to decide what memorabilia to collect, or to prophesy what the future will think of folk idols of today. In the 1950s, how many diligently charted the path of Elvis Presley, searching out posters or signed photographs, cherishing discarded clothing or accumulating discs? Who would have thought that the early scratchy recordings of Caruso are now worth a good deal of money?

In 1987 Charlie Chaplin's hat, cane and shoes made £110,000 (more than $170,000) at auction. The intrinsic value of these items was nil, and popular as he always was, it would need great imagination to predict the ultimate worth of his props. Even two canes, without real authentication, made £5,000 and £1,600 (about $7,750 and $2,500).

Similarly, when Walt Disney was making his very first cartoons, none of his animators had the foresight to put the artwork in bank vaults (where they should have been, judging by present-day demand). Nor were the cheap Mickey Mouse tin toys loved

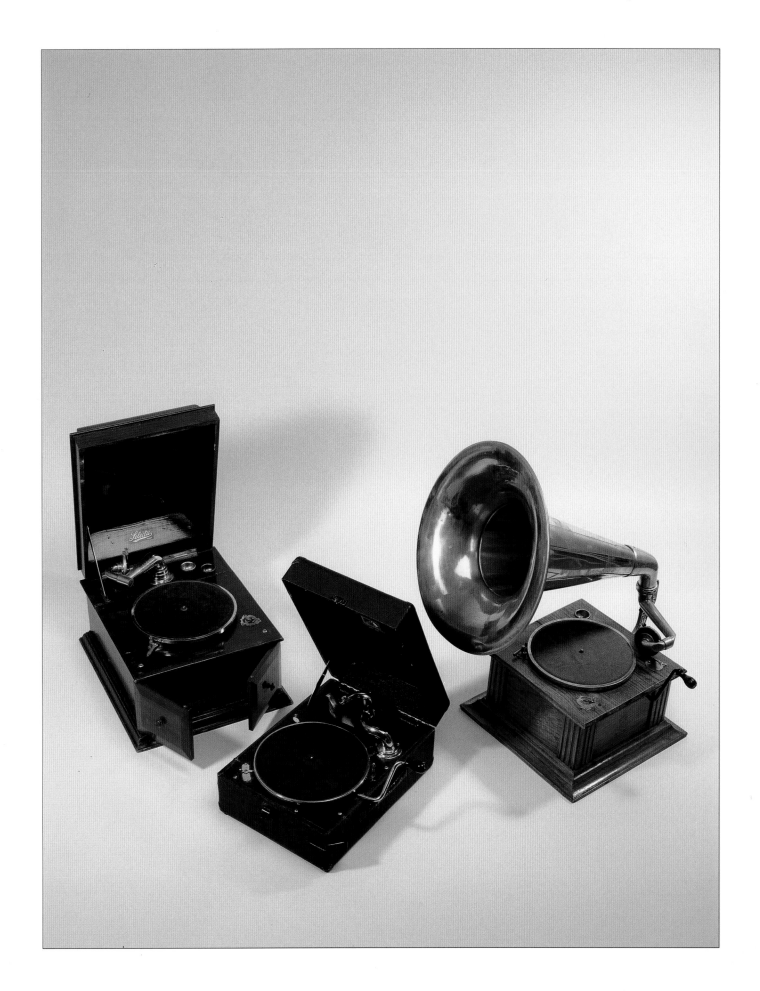

The values of old golf clubs have soared in recent years, but there is difficulty in determining their age as they remained unchanged over many decades. The maker's name is often the clue. Drivers have probably changed less than irons.

Inset:

The introduction of dimpled golf balls early in this century spelled an end to experiment. The earliest golf-balls were made of feathers compressed in a leather outer covering; gutta-percha (rubber) balls, "gutties", were first used about 1850. These early golf balls fetch four figures.

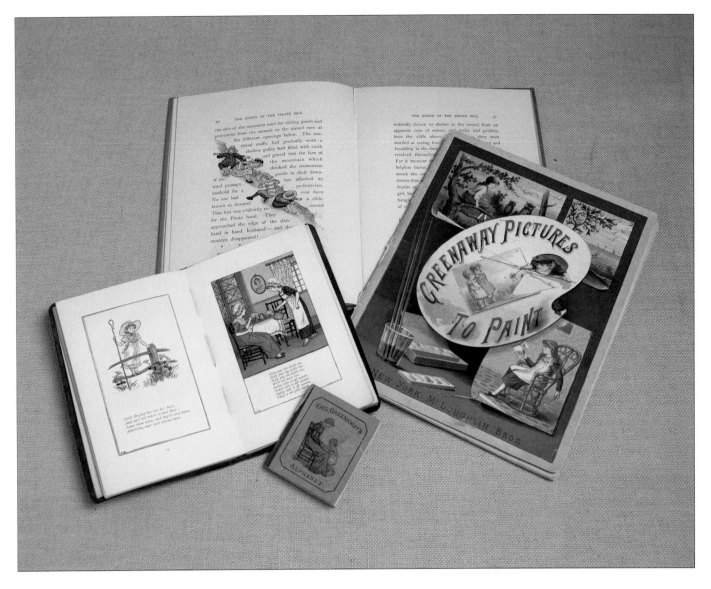

and cherished, or, as today's collectors want, kept in their boxes.

What is the most valuable magazine in the world? Probably *Beeton's Christmas Annual* of 1887. Why? Because it featured *A Study in Scarlet,* the first Sherlock Holmes story, and most of the copies of a very nondescript magazine were thrown away. A car carburettor dating from around 1900 would have been discarded if it had gone wrong; today it is worth more than £200 (more than $300). As for 1920s and 1930s travel posters, stuck on railway stations or in subways, the best examples regularly top four figures. It might be thought that these are totally exceptional; but they are not. Everything has a value. It is up to a collector to determine how much.

This applies to all antiques, pictures, sporting antiques – early gutta-percha golf balls (1850 on) and one-off clubs command huge amounts. But remember, too, that some antiques have resolutely refused to live up to their expectations, and this includes, notably, prints. And there is a reason. The photocopier and computer scanner have made them suspect.

Perhaps there is one golden rule. If it is difficult to make then it is difficult to fake!

Above: Early children's books are greatly sought after, those of Kate Greenaway (1846-1901) especially so. She was never difficult to imitate and fakes abound.

Buying

A decorous art nouveau lamp. These were sometimes in bronze and sometimes in spelter (zinc) which ages badly, and is often treated so as to appear to be bronze. Unobtrusive scratching with the finger nail will reveal all!

ollecting is passing through an exciting transitional stage, and many dealers and collectors have not yet come to grips with it. Since World War II there have been three basic phases. Up to the early 1960s antique collecting was a minority hobby and a complete mystery to those on the outside. Most people shied away from antique shops, puzzled and bewildered, and few had never been inside an auction room. If they possessed antiques of value, handed down from their parents or grandparents, they did not know about them.

All this altered when television began to run regular programmes on antiques, and viewers realized that there was big money in objects that they might well have around the house. Viewing figures were

high, and millions of people began to peck around, buying this and that, not knowing what they were doing but getting a good deal of fun out of it. They were catered for by not only the old-time dealers but thousands of amateurs, who did not know very much about antiques either, but were willing to invest a few pounds or dollars in taking a stall in one or other of the antique markets that were being opened everywhere. These were supplemented by antique fairs and flea markets, as well as by the open markets that have existed in Britain since the Middle Ages.

At about the same time there was a huge demand abroad, particularly in Australia, for European, and especially British, antiques, and the "shipper" appeared. These dealers had vast warehouses, to whom

A simple hanging box of some age, country-made (the dovetailing is crude), and probably a church candle-holder, though without provenance no-one can definitely be certain. This applies to much early oak and even Victorian pine.

ABCDEFGHIJKLMNOPQRSTVUWXYZ

Lord may every rising sun
See a better life begun
May I love and serve thee more
Than I ever lov'd before
In my work and in my play
Be thou Lord with me to day

Hannah Green
Aged 12 Years
1835

dealers and "runners" – go-betweens who made a living buying from one dealer and selling to another – took their booty, often bought from the semi-amateurs at knock-down prices.

The low value of the British pound in relation to many other currencies encouraged buyers from the rest of Europe and from North America to come to Britain to buy. The Japanese had not yet fully entered the antique scene, and other nations of the Pacific Rim were only marginal participants, although they would increasingly be as European countries faced their own economic difficulties. In the 1960s anything and everything had a market. This euphoric state of affairs could not last. Semi-amateur dealers, who had learned nothing and forgotten nothing, made one mistake too many and over-extended themselves. Even long-established antique dealers went dramatically out of business when the price of silver collapsed in the 1970s.

However, the antique trade survived. Some amateurs learned and managed to cope with changing times and the need to discriminate or specialize. It was gradually becoming a buyer's market, in which goods in the lower or middle ranges could stay on a dealer's stall or in a shop almost indefinitely. There was always, and there always is, a demand for the highest quality, and the prices of the very best pieces continued to rise until they became out of reach to all but the very rich.

The third stage has been relatively short, and dates from about

Above: Teapots of this quality were usually of silver. Early teapots were quite small, as tea was immensely expensive and kept in locked containers to stop the servants getting at it. In the nineteenth century simple-minded forgers produced "Elizabethan teapots" - when tea was not known!

Opposite: Every young lady sewed samplers, and invariably dated them. Many are true art works, decorative, naive, and moving. When the young lady became an old lady the dates were often taken out, so that no-one could determine the maker's age! Highly collected, and much faked, so that minor damage is sometimes welcomed as evidence of authenticity.

Above: Beware of mirrors! Old picture frames are used to provide a surround to modern mirror glass (which is cheap), spots are difficult to take out, resilvering is expensive, and large wall-size mirrors are incredibly fragile. To establish authenticity, put the thumb-nail to the surface of the mirror; early mirror glass is thin, and this shows in the reflection. The glass on this mirror is modern bevelled glass.

Opposite: A Worcester soup tureen of good quality, as is the case with most Worcester porcelain, a generic name for a number of companies such as Chamberlain and Grainger. Royal Worcester, still in existence, was established in 1862.

1990, when recession began to bite. People became fearful of the future, and spent their money on necessities or hung on to it for dark days ahead. Antique dealers began to drop away like flies, and the shippers either shut up shop or closed part of their premises.

Dealers, who in the past had been accustomed to "double up" – buying something for a hundred dollars or pounds and expecting two hundred for it – found that they had to be content with a more modest profit. They were often desperate to sell, seeing the fate of their colleagues, many of whom had "done a runner" (shut up shop one night, and then decamped without leaving a forwarding address).

Throughout the entire period from the early 1960s onwards, the auction rooms were largely buoyant. The London-based auction houses opened offices in New York and later in the new outlets of Japan and Hong Kong. Old-established auctioneers were taken over by the major players, which now had an additional source of revenue. Previously they only charged the vendor commission. They then also began to charge the buyer commission, which averaged 10 per cent.

So we arrive at the collecting scene today. It is transitional, largely because of the great social changes that have taken place in recent

years and that have yet to be fully evaluated. In the past, antiques were collected to furnish a family house or to confer status. Among low-income groups these "antiques" would be novelty items, often of porcelain or pottery, bought from seaside resorts and placed in display cabinets or on mantelpieces. They would serve the same purpose as Dresden figures in a high-income home.

But a family house of even twenty years ago is not the family house of today. Families, of whatever socio-economic level, have less interest in displaying little treasures. With a premium on time, the accent is on efficiency, plain surfaces and ease of management. The pretty ornament has less and less appeal in the multi-media age, where more attention is paid to a television screen or VDU. Fine furniture is less regarded, even unnoticed; it will not cause envy among friends and neighbours, among whom there is far more interest in something comfortable and useful.

The collector today is not an endangered species, but he or she is certainly no longer a buy-anything-and-stick-it-on-a-shelf person. Those days are gone for good, although there are still many who will buy the occasional new figurine at a ridiculously low price – £2 ($3) or so – more from habit than from any other reason. The collector today is more focused and more selective.

There are several kinds of collector interested in affordable antiques. The most obvious is the collector who wants to make a

Above: A George II wine cooler, mahogany with brass banding, the kind of small antique that will always be desirable, though not often used for its original purpose.

Opposite: A fine early-nineteenth-century beech and elm Windsor chair. The arm-rests and the stretchers were bent under steam. Elm was used for the seat. Comfortable and unpretentious, the Windsor chair is a true classic (and easily repaired) and is still being made using the old methods, which date back to 1724.

Opposite: A collection of fine paperweights, evolved in Venice in the early nineteenth century and spreading to France via Bohemia about 1845. Three French firms dominate the paperweight market, and clever fakes abound, often difficult to detect as glass ages very little.

profit, of turning an affordable antique into an unaffordable one. There is the collector who is interested in one particular object or group of objects, who has as much joy in the pursuit as in the capture. And there is the collector who is entranced by some beautiful object, who often comes across it unawares, and who will purchase it at almost any cost.

The true collector has to establish ground rules. It is vitally important to know something about what you are collecting, and there is no better way than seeing the item and handling it. This is not possible in museums, but it is in antique outlets and on viewing days in auctions. This is perhaps the best way, even if there is no intention to buy. It can lead to a long-term learning process, before a collection is actually started, and the process can be intensely enjoyable. The accumulation of knowledge usually is.

It would be impertinent to suggest to the reader what he or she should collect. It would, however, be sensible for a would-be collector to make a decision on whether the coveted objects should be a collection, to be amassed and displayed, or whether they should be part of a life-style that will, if necessary, be used or become part of the surroundings, rather than admired and looked at. A collection can be

Below: A mahogany Canterbury originally used mainly for sheet music, but equally suitable as a magazine rack. It was made in all woods, including bamboo and, in the Victorian period, walnut, and often fetch more money - up to £4000 ($6200) in satinwood - than they are really worth.

made of a group of items, such as old kitchen equipment or "office" antiques – pens, inkstands, paperweights, maybe even old typewriters and telephones – that actually have a function and serve a purpose.

There is no purpose in collecting items that are simply boring. There is little to be said for modern commemorative plates, first-day postal covers or limited editions of figurines by famous factories. It is an easy way out, but the supply of these items is governed by demand, which is high, and this has the perverse effect that so many are made that their collecting value is no more, usually considerably less, than the buying price.

Anything that is in demand is faked. Fakes are often difficult to detect, and even when they are crude they often fool the buyer simply because he or she wants to believe that they are genuine. How can a fake be recognized? Often never. Fakes and forgeries fill the museums

Above: Stamp collecting became popular soon after the first postage stamp, the Penny Black, was issued in 1840. Stamps are often produced by small nations for collectors to supplement the country's economy.

Opposite: Canteens of cutlery are common, and are often bought for use rather than for show as they are inexpensive. They date from the middle of the nineteenth century, and sometimes include grape-scissors, sugar-tongs, and other knick-knacks. Silver-handled cutlery can often be deceptively heavy - wafer-thin silver on a resin base.

Above: A Georgian tray-top commode, useful as a bedside table. The word commode has various meanings, and can describe many different articles of furniture. From 1851 it became used to describe a container for a chamber-pot.

Opposite: A Parian figure of a girl signed J.B. Kirk of Dublin. Parian was unglazed porcelain, and it was an attempt to imitate marble. It was immensely popular in the Victorian period. Unglazed porcelain is also known as bisque.

of the world. It is important to know the real thing, and instinct can often be as valuable as experience and knowledge. Early nineteenth-century Staffordshire figures, often made by illiterate women and children for fairs and markets and sold for just a few pence, were being faked within fifty years. These are now over a century old, and have all the requisite signs of age.

When you are selecting a category to collect – that is, if your choice is cold-blooded and not spontaneous – it is sensible to consider the chances of the items in which you are interested being faked. Some antiques are too complicated to fake – fine early watches, for example – some are made of material which ages imperceptibly and cannot be satisfactorily copied, and other items are not worth faking – yet. The more obscure an object and the less valuable it is, the less chance there is of its being faked.

Left: A ladies' writing table in rosewood from about 1820. Coal was now being used in many households, and as this gave out more heat than wood ladies' complexions had to be protected. So ladies' writing tables were often fitted with screens. They were not altogether functional, giving only a small writing area.

Antiques can be collected because they are often cheaper than their present-day equivalent and better made. Typical of this group is 1930s furniture, which often employs marvellous walnut and mahogany veneer (and does it matter if it is backed by five-ply wood?) However, functional 1930s furniture for the home, which often looks as though it has escaped from an office, is faked and foisted on us with the name of a famous designer of the period.

Similarly, 1950s furniture can be obtained very cheaply, is often very stylish and well-made and should enjoy the status of 1950s automobiles – but it does not. The same applies to many 1950s bits and pieces (known in the antique trade as "smalls"), although for beginners it is easy to confuse the 1930s and 1950s styles. A way to get to know the difference is to go to a library and look at the advertisements in 1930s and 1950s magazines.

Buying can be fun. It can also be a nightmare. Sitting in on an auction without intent to buy will give you a feel for how auctions work and will also give you a guide to current prices and even fads and fancies. Always buy a catalogue, make a note of interesting pieces and, if you are buying, note against the lot you are considering the top price you are prepared to go. If you scratch your nose and fear that it may be interpreted as an indication that you are buying, do

Opposite: An Edwardian satinwood bed with caned front and back, painted oval panels, and banding and stringing of rosewood, boxwood, and ivory.

Above: Doulton Lambeth jardiniere and two vases, decorated in her distinctive style by Hannah Barlow, and made some time between 1880 and 1892.

Opposite: A fascinating array of artefacts. The most interesting is the phrenological bust in which the brain is mapped out into divisions. Phrenology dates from 1815. The rack contains chemical equipment - in the Victorian period chemistry was a popular hobby. The leather Gladstone bag was introduced in 1882.

not worry; signs and twitches are the mark of the buyer who is known to the auctioneer. Occasionally, you may be puzzled to see that, although no one seems to be bidding, the auctioneer carries on upping the price. He is taking bids "off the wall" or "off the chandelier", to get bids up to the reserve figure. If there is no reserve, he may have to backtrack. Telephone bidding from non-existent callers is also a feature of the auction scene that may trap the unwary into paying more than they need.

Buying privately can be hazardous. Dealers often pretend to be ordinary householders and deal from their homes, and a garage sale may not be what it appears. Dealers who work from a shop or known premises have their reputation to think of. If a considerable amount of money is changing hands, it is a good idea to ask for a detailed description of the piece and a receipt. A receipt will not be given at an open fair or market, and a receipt will not serve as a guarantee. It is buyer beware, especially as stolen property is often disposed of at such events, and purchase of an item does not give title to it.

Most dealers, unless they are very elevated indeed, expect to haggle and should be prepared to take off anything up to 25 per cent, perhaps more, of the marked price. A dealer will prefer to be made an offer rather than give a price.

Always examine a prospective purchase very closely for signs of damage, and here a sense of touch is often more sure than sight. Even experienced dealers fail to do this. A very low-priced item can mean that the piece is flawed, the dealer is cutting his or her losses, and what might seem a bargain can be a terrible mistake for an innocent private buyer.

PHRENOLOGY
BY
L.N. FOWLER

Selling

Opposite: Musical instruments form a vast collecting area, though there are pitfalls for the novice. "Old" violins with "old" labels, visible beneath the strings, were manufactured in quantity during the Victorian period with intent to deceive. Some antique instruments in perfect working order are cheaper than new ones, especially those such as harmoniums which are heavy to move!

Below: Three Art Deco porcelain figures made in Austria, of great charm and period interest, still available today at very little cost.

All those who really do collect and are not just amassing a large collection will, as their knowledge grows and their taste is refined, find that they will want to trade in some of their earlier buys for something better. They may be mistakes – pieces bought early in a collecting career – or they may be inferior examples, or it may be that the collector is taking a different direction.

Selling is very different from buying, and if the collector bought the antique at the going rate, a loss must be expected when selling it on, unless it was bought years before or at a time when the antique was unfashionable or unrecognized. It also depends whether the item was bought from a dealer or an auction house; if it was bought from an auction house, it is possible that it was bought at less than it was worth. (Worth, in the context of antiques and collectables, depends entirely on what people are prepared to pay; there is no such thing as a recommended retail price.) If it was bought cheaply it probably means that the collector has more knowledge than any general dealers who may have been present. A general dealer has to know a bit about everything and cannot be expected to know all there is to know about an out-of-the-way antique or a narrow field to which a collector has given a good deal of attention and acquired considerable expertise. Knowledge is power in the world of collecting.

When it come to selling, much will depend on what the article is. If it is obscure, the average dealer, asked to give a price, will often be nonplussed and will probably suggest a low price. A dealer who

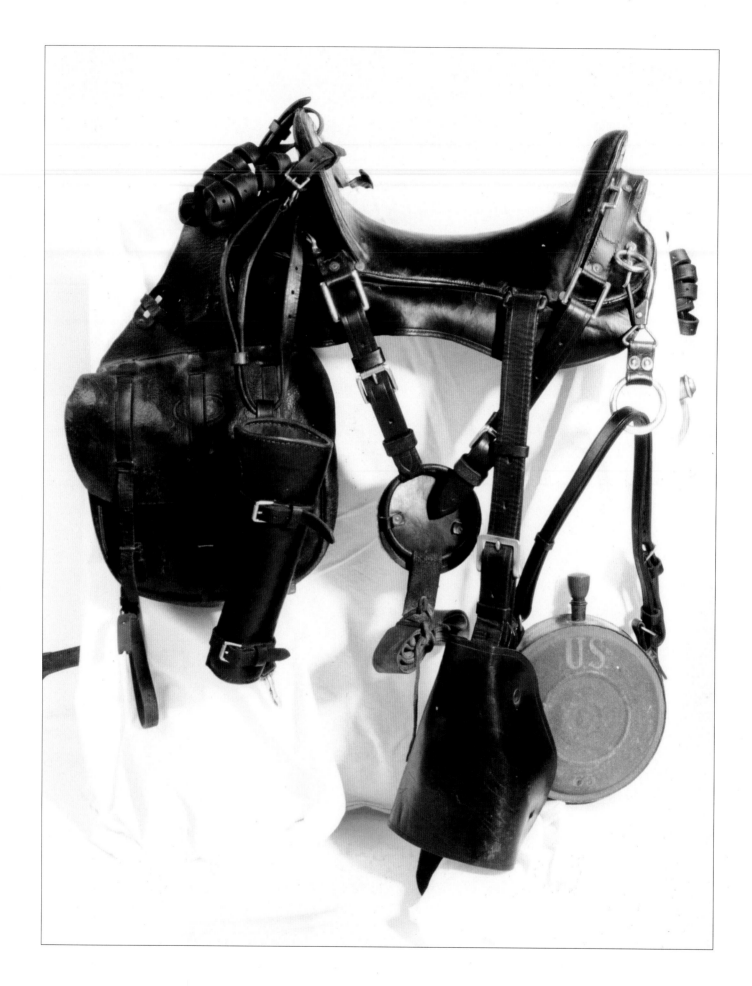

offers a high price for something he or she does not know the value of will shortly be going out of business.

Specialist dealers, rather than general antique dealers, should be approached if you are selling out of the ordinary items, but outside the big cities these are few and far between. It is, therefore, better to consider an auction house. At one time antique dealers were regularly visited by members of the public with antiques to sell, and it was one of the reasons why, despite the much higher overheads, they were so keen to have a shop rather than a stall at an antiques fair or market. Some dealers were honest, looking for a sensible mark-up, but others were unscrupulous, giving a fraction of what the article was worth. As the public became more aware of auction houses and discovered that they were not as awesome as they at first thought, the auction house became the natural place to which to take items. If they were of such low quality that the auction room would not take them, which was often the case, only then would an antique dealer be approached. Naturally the dealer would not be told that the piece or pieces had been rejected for auction. "Privates" or "punters" can be every bit as unscrupulous as dealers.

Selling at auction is absolutely painless. A reserve should be agreed with the auctioneer, so that the item will not be given away or bought at a low price by a "ring", a group of dealers who band together, do not bid against each other and appoint a spokesman to buy on their behalf as cheaply as possible. The items are then auctioned within the ring, and the difference between the price paid at auction and the price paid in the "knock out" is divided among the members of the ring (except for the dealer who has finally acquired the goods). This is illegal but there is no way to stop it, especially as, in Britain, it is legal for two dealers to work in concert. In shady auctions, the auctioneer himself can be involved in the ring, so an auction house should be selected very carefully and a "back street" outfit should be avoided.

Some auctioneers make a charge if the object fails to sell at a price above the agreed reserve, but it is not common. Many auctions charge a minimum commission whatever price the lot makes in the sale-room. It is important to find this out before putting in the goods, as well as the rate of the commission, which can be up to 15 per cent but is usually less. When fixing the reserve, it must be remembered that the buyer, too, has to pay a premium, usually of 10 per cent or so, and this amount might make the difference between a sale and a no-sale.

There is one area where the difference between a buying price and a selling price is almost painfully wide, and that is books, especially "trade" books, the general stock of a second-hand bookshop. This is not due to greed on the part of the bookseller, even though he or she may mark up the book by several hundred per cent, but because the turnover of even the successful book dealers is low. From a stock of several thousand books there may be individual books that wait years for a buyer.

There is always the option of selling privately to fellow enthusiasts. Collectors specializing in a class of antiques are often drawn together by a kind of grapevine, or are catered for by specialist newsletters. Often this is preferred; it keeps the item, as it were, in the family.

Opposite: The type of antique which can be worth almost anything, and to an American redolent of the days of the Wild West.

Repairs &
Renovations

Repairing antiques can be as simple or as time-consuming as anyone could wish. But the general advice is – don't. A bad repair detracts from something that, despite faults, can be beautiful or has value, and a repair can always be spotted by someone. A seemingly perfect repair to a piece of china can be instantly seen by the use of ultraviolet light, a cheap aid possessed by everyone who is involved in china and pottery. If a dealer has repairs done or does them him or herself, and they are discovered, immediately all the stock is suspect.

A collector, of course, can repair or not repair as he or she wants. If it is a "life-style" antique, there are no objections, but many collectors prefer the object to be just as it is, imperfections and all. Damage can reduce the value of an item, but not necessarily. There are certain early objects, such as artefacts from ancient Greece or Rome, where damage is expected and where restoration is allowed.

Cleaning is a different matter, and an antique of almost any kind looks better for being clean. It is important to know what cleaner to use. In general, proprietary cleaners do their job very well, and for certain tasks soap and water cannot be improved upon. Soap and water can be used to clean amber, horn and tortoiseshell. Ivory should be sponged with water, but never soaked. Gold can be cleaned

Opposite: A silver and cut-glass cruet set with a thistle motif, therefore of Scottish origin. Novelty and sporting cruet sets (especially those connected with golf) are not uncommon.

Below: Character jugs have come a long way since the humble Toby jug, made to celebrate a well-known toper. These are World War I famous figures, and together they are very rare. Single figures from this Royal Staffordshire set are available at reasonable prices.

Opposite: William and Mary chairs from about 1690 in walnut with cane seats and back. They strongly show the influence of Dutch furniture; William of Orange came from Holland. This style was transitional, and the ugly arches beneath the seat were soon discarded. In fifty years mahogany would oust walnut and the other traditional woods, and show how furniture could be made.

Below: Antique ring and bracelet. Jewellery was often in complicated sets, which could be split up according to the occasion. There were strict rules governing jewellery; diamonds were for the evening, and displaying them during the daytime could be reckoned vulgar.

with soap and water, and finished off with jeweller's rouge, a polishing powder of hydrated ferric oxide. White marble can be cleaned with soap and water, but coloured marble should be tackled with gasoline, as should alabaster (very similar to marble but considerably softer and not so valuable).

Ammonia is a reliable cleaning agent. It helps to remove the tarnish on silver, and, when diluted with warm water, cleans porcelain and glass. Strong ammonia strips varnish, and brass responds well, and can be finished off with a vinegar and salt mixture. Bronze should be treated with caution; as a result of years of corrosion it acquires a greenish coating called patina, which adds to its appeal, so much so that patina is faked by making a solution of copper nitrate and salt, followed by a mixture made up of 100 parts of weak vinegar, 5 parts of ammonium chloride and 1 part of oxalic acid. This takes a week to come into effect, and although impressive, the tendency of the faker is to spread the mixture too evenly, whereas true patination is erratic. The clever faker who distributes his mixture at random is also caught out; the untreated bronze does not look right. If genuine, it should be part way to the patination stage.

Opposite: A fine carriage clock by Matthew Norman of London. The practice of showing the movement was exaggerated with the skeleton clock, which is a clock without a case under a glass dome.

Right: A selection of Georgian coins. Condition is vitally important in the collection of coins (numismatics), and old coins, such as those of ancient Rome, are not necessarily valuable. A Georgian penny in rubbed condition is virtually worthless.

Pewter can be polished using whiting or silver sand, but great care should be taken because the metal is very soft, and there is always the danger of taking off the "touches" or makers' marks. Iron should be treated with caution, using fine wire-wool and oil; automobile rust remover is another option, if it used sensibly. It is often advisable to halt the corrosion, rather than obliterate it. It is easier to over-clean than under-clean.

Objects that have been buried for some time, such as old coins, often acquire a limestone accretion. It is possible to clean them by coating any visible surfaces with paraffin wax and then dipping the item into concentrated nitric acid. This can be dangerous and you must wear protective clothing, including gloves and goggles. The acid attacks the limestone without getting at the object. When all the limestone has gone, the paraffin wax is removed, and the piece can be washed under running water.

Choices have to be made. When microscopes or other brass objects were made, lacquer was often applied to the brass, and over the years this has got grubby, detracting from the look of the piece. Acetone

A selection of mugs and drinking glasses, some engraved. Glasses bearing Jacobite engravings - concerning the eighteenth-century rising of the Scots under Bonnie Prince Charlie - are very valuable and often faked. Drinking glasses with chipped rims are often ground down to appear perfect, best detected with the finger tip rather than by the eye.

(nail-polish remover) will remove the lacquer, but if there is a change of mind the application of kerosene (paraffin oil) will halt the action. Commonsense will often give a clue as to what not to use.

You should never allow water near plaster of Paris (not greatly used in antiques) or gesso, the substance used in old ornate picture frames and often moulded around patterns of wire on a wooden base.

No one would argue that scratches on glass are other than a nuisance and should be dealt with. A chamois leather impregnated with jeweller's rouge will help. Cloudy glass can be cleaned with 5 per cent sodium hydroxide in water. Interior glass clouding, as in a decanter, can be infuriating because it cannot be reached, even by a bottle-brush. Decanters are usually bought for use rather than display, and cloudiness is simply not wanted. There are two methods that usually work – swilling coarse sand around inside the decanter or rattling around the lead shot of the kind used by anglers. It is very much trial and error, but as glass itself is very resilient a cocktail of fluids may succeed where everything else has failed.

The most potent area for restorers is china and pottery, and if the urge cannot be resisted it is wise to know that the worst colour to imitate is white. There are thousands of shades of white, and pat-

A silver part table service, London 1853, comprising seventeen each table forks, dessert forks, teaspoons, eighteen dessert spoons, eight table spoons, six salt spoons, five coffee spoons, four sauce ladles, two mustard spoons, one basting spoon, one butter knife,a sifter spoon and a pair of sugar tongs.

terned areas are simple compared with the difficulty of getting the right white. Often china or pottery with damage looks bad because of the dirt in the cracks, rather than the crack itself, which is often not seen with a superficial glance. Dirt in a crack may be removed by cotton wool dipped in bleach. For articles of no great value, the porcelain or pottery can be immersed in a solution of household bleach, but there is a danger with doing this, because the crack may be wider than first thought and the removal of the dirt may cause the object to disintegrate, although putting it together again using instant fixative is an option. A previous repair may have been done when only one of the older glues was available; the present-day repairer has a much wider armoury. There are many materials for repairs to porcelain and pottery on the market, many of them convincing.

Furniture can be freshened up with a solution of vinegar and water, polished, using a good proprietary make or a mixture of beeswax and turpentine (three parts to eight), or French polished. Think carefully before French polishing, because the process is not as old as many think. At one time it was the fashion to French polish anything and everything, and it may be that you will have to remove the French polish from a piece of furniture by using liquid ammonia and acetone.

81

Opposite: An elaborate display cabinet or vitrine, a product of the nineteenth-century desire to display small items. They can be very elaborate, comprising mirrors, often oddly shaped, and large expanses of glass. They can look ungainly, as in this example, or overbearing as in the late-Victorian ebonised vitrines, where decoration runs riot, and which until recently were regarded as monstrosities.

No valuable piece of furniture should be repaired without contemplating the consequences, and although expert restoration is readily available it is not cheap and the cost may outstrip the value of the piece of furniture. A structural fault may be remedied without it being seen, although it may devalue the furniture if it is done crudely. Dealers have been known almost to dismantle a piece of furniture in the sale-room if it is in any way suspect. The structure of "carcase" furniture – chests of drawers, for example – is more easily repaired than show furniture, although if there is surface damage, such as peeling or damaged veneer, it will need expert attention.

It may seem a simple matter to replace veneer, but it is likely that the veneer itself will be complex. It is probable that the surfaces, such as the fronts of drawers, will have surrounds, which can be made in a multitude of geometric forms, each tiny piece slotted in like a jigsaw, and this is work for a cabinet-maker and not an amateur, even a skilled amateur. Modern veneer is much thinner than old veneer, and two layers may need to be applied where one was enough before.

Whatever their capabilities, most antique dealers will at some time have tried their hands at simple repairs – putting back a chair leg, replacing a broken chair stretcher or sticking back veneer that has lifted, but you must always remember that a poor repair is worse

Right: A Queen Anne walnut bureau. The design was taken over by the mahogany furniture makers. The quality of a bureau can be gauged by the fitted interior beneath the fall front, which can be a marvel of craftsmanship with secret drawers and superb detail.

Opposite: A curious and uninspired corner cupboard. Corner cupboards were early ventures into display cabinets where the owner kept his little treasures. Glass was too expensive to use except for the very rich, and could only be made in small panels (the glass of antique mirrors is often in two sections).

Below: A three-seater sofa of no great age, with a shell-shaped back. After World War I there was a desire for comfort and chintz, and the three-piece suite of a sofa and two armchairs made its debut, and no home was complete without it.

than useless. Old repairs, however, are often acceptable and can even add to the charm of a piece, but the furniture itself must be pre-eighteenth century.

If repairs are undertaken the right kind of wood should be used. Some woods, such as tulip-wood and zebra-wood, are almost unobtainable today, and rosewood is scarce. Structural repairs that seem to be in character – many pieces were originally made with supporting blocks to take the strain, for example – often betray themselves by lack of thought to detail, such as the use of round-headed screws.

If repairs are undertaken, old-fashioned glue called Scotch glue, sold in blocks, and heated in a double metal pot, should be used. Never use instant glue or impact adhesive, so that you can be sure that in any future repairs the process can be reversed – Scotch glue can be melted.

Stuffed furniture should, of course, be re-upholstered if the original is either sagging or the outer material needs replacing. If it is Victorian furniture, it may merely need new webbing, which holds the spring and the stuffing (horse-hair) in place. The stuffing can either be replaced with new horse hair or a substitute material such as kapok can be used. This task is not so simple as it sounds, and an immense amount of horse-hair can be compressed in the most modest

Opposite: A presentation of moths and butterflies.

Overleaf left: Porcelain reached its peak in the nineteenth century, and the skills will never be recaptured - nor the risks attempted. In certain types of porcelain a vase could take weeks to make - and could then crumble in the kiln.

Overleaf right: The Boston rocker was a variant on the English Windsor chair. Curiously the rocking chair was never taken up by the British, and possibly the reasons are climatic and architectural - British houses rarely had verandahs.

Below: A classic pair of library steps, which, when folded, was transformed into a very handsome chair.

of chairs and it is inevitably filthy. Upholstery can be very rewarding, but if the shape is complex, as in a nineteenth-century *chaise longue* or day-bed, it can be quite difficult and take a long time. If you are in any doubt, seek professional help or advice.

The question of woodworm is simple. If a piece has woodworm holes, shake it and see if wood dust trickles out. This indicates that the woodworm is alive. It can be treated if the appropriate remedy is pumped into the holes immediately. Old woodworm holes, where there is no danger of infestation, can be filled with a mixture of beeswax and turpentine, and then suitable coloured to tone in with the wood (shoe polish is often used in the antique trade).

Paintings have their own problems. Oil paintings can be cleaned using a proprietary cleaner, which can be very effective if the instructions are carefully followed. Stop work as soon as the cotton-wool to which the cleaner is applied begins to colour. Old watercolours are sometimes foxed – that is, they bear small brown marks caused by damp. The marks can be taken out using a solution of hydrogen peroxide and alcohol applied with a camel-hair brush. This is a delicate business, and where the paper has faded anyway it needs a sure eye to blend the restoration with the original. And this applies to all forms of restoration. When in doubt, leave as it is.

Posterity will thank you.

Tricks of the Trade

Opposite: A lacquered table of indeterminate date. Lacquering in the Chinese style was a popular hobby of the 1920s, and much good furniture was ruined by well-intentioned amateurs, the heirs of those who French-varnished anything which stood still.

Below: A fine old oak chest, with deep satisfying carving, rugged no-nonsense feet, and a bowed top which no-one has misguidedly tried to straighten out. Old oak is the Cinderella of antiques - still grossly undervalued.

The antique dealer's aim is to sell, and a few are not too scrupulous how they do it. There is a thin line between faking and doctoring or improving. In the past, the true antique dealer was mainly concerned with furniture, but changing conditions, in particular available space and money, have meant that the dealer has to cover a wider field, although many of the elite dealers use china and other small antiques merely to decorate the furniture, and if these pieces sell, so much the better.

FURNITURE

One of the tricks of the furniture trade is to simulate age. This applies particularly to old oak dating from the seventeenth century or earlier. Oak is one of the strongest of woods, and can take any amount of rough treatment. The construction of oak chests was often

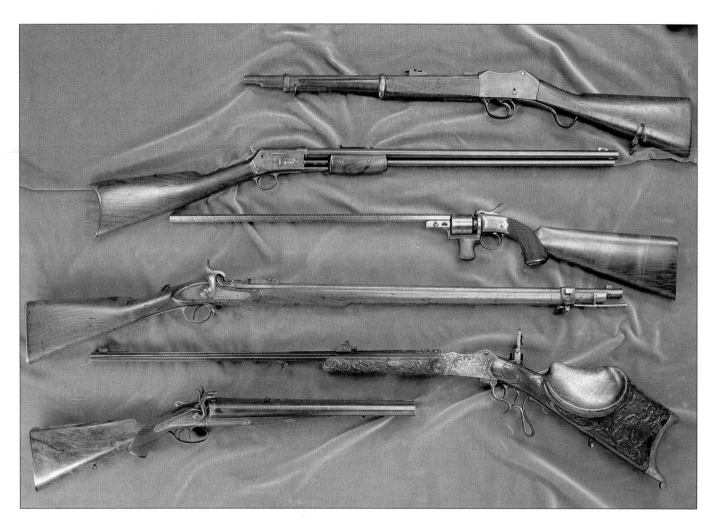

Above: A fine collection of weaponry of various dates. The flintlock (using a flint striking powder on a cap) and the matchlock persisted into almost modern times, despite the introduction of the percussion mechanism still in use today. It is a restricted branch of collecting in Britain due to strenuously enforced firearms laws.

Opposite: A walnut chest-on-chest from about 1720. Over the years many of these have been divided into two separate pieces of furniture. The chest-on-chest was a curious concept as no-one could reach the upper drawers except on a chair.

crude and quite easy to emulate. If the oak itself was new and had to be aged, it was a simple matter to make the chest and leave it in the open for a year or two. To bruise the wood and give the impression of hard usage, the chests would be hit with chains. It was not unknown for "old oak" to be buried in the garden and then dug up and cleaned. The feet of real old oak chests, chairs and tables were often damaged by water and wear, and this had to be imitated.

It is easy enough to reproduce the effects of age, except to an expert, but it is not so easy to provide convincing fittings, such as locks and hinges. Hinges did not matter so much, because the earliest hinges were no more than bent, thick wire that wore out and was replaced, often within a fairly short space of time, usually by T-shaped hinges, which were equally simple to fake. Locks were a different matter, however. Together with firearms, locks were, in terms of technology, ahead of almost every other artefact, with the notable exception of clocks and watches. It is not surprising that many "old" chests lack their locks. It reduces their value, but not to an enormous extent. Gullible private buyers are told that they were broken off when the chests were stolen and broken into, or the key or keys – some chests had three locks – were lost.

In the 1960s old walnut Spanish chests were very popular. Astute dealers went to rural areas of Spain, where walnut chests were being made in exactly the same manner as they had been made several cen-

turies before, and brought them back to Britain. Nothing much needed doing to them. There was increasing interest in seventeenth-century walnut and eighteenth-century mahogany furniture, and they would be doctored, making saleable something that would otherwise stay in stock for a long time.

Desirable though it was, the more spectacular pieces of Victorian furniture were rarely faked because it was too time-consuming to do so, even if the expertise was there. The four-poster bed was also shunned – the cost of the wood was too much to make it worthwhile. Some pieces of furniture were more popular than others. Items were converted, or made up from different pieces of furniture (this is called a "marriage"). Chests-on-chests (several layers of drawers, one on top of the other so that the top surface is way above eye level) were cut down to make two pieces of furniture. There was one problem here; because the top surface could not be seen, it was not veneered, so veneer had to be applied. There was a demand, especially in America, for small tables called sofa tables, and these were dutifully made, using parts from genuine eighteenth-century pieces.

Some doctoring is allowable. If a "long" set of chairs is bought and some are damaged it is acceptable to spread the imperfect compo-

A superb early-Victorian rosewood balloon-back chair with elegant and unusual legs. The balloon-back lasted for many decades.

nents around so that they are less noticeable. Cannibalization is also common. If a dealer buys five chairs, one can be rejected and used for spare parts to make up a set of four, or made up to six, using outside material. A set of six is infinitely more desirable than a set of four. Odd numbers are non-starters.

Reproduction furniture, often of high quality, can be represented as original by using faded polish or by a little clever damage, not enough to reduce the value but to convince a would-be buyer that this is the original article. This can be a complicated process, however, because over the generations many owners have tried to "improve" their furniture. This may merely mean swapping over feet or handles to make the furniture more fashionable, but it can be more integral to the piece. In the nineteenth century, for example, fragments of early oak panels were built into contemporary sideboards, and such additions sometimes confuse.

Many dealers' recasting of old furniture is often ill-advised, because fashions alter, and furniture that has been cut-down or otherwise mutilated suddenly finds itself in fashion – in the original form. Eighteenth- and nineteenth-century linen presses (mahogany wardrobes with drawers instead of hanging room) were bought pure-

Victorian hand-painted papier-mâché trays. Papier mâché ("chewed paper") was evolved in the Far East, introduced to France and reaching Britain about 1750, where it proved immensely popular for well over a century, not only for small items but for tables, chairs, and even a piano. Mother-of-pearl was introduced to combine with the painting, which was often carried out by very talented artists.

Above: A high-quality doll's house of recent date. As in all dolls' houses the age can be judged by the fittings and especially the wallpaper.

Opposite: Screens were used for a variety of purposes - as room dividers, to ensure privacy, and, in small sizes, to reduce the heat of an open fire, often believed to be harmful to ladies' complexions. All materials were used - paper in Japan, leather and fabrics in Europe and America, as well as bamboo, a lightweight wood making it easy to move the screen around. This one is of leather. Screens were often covered with "scraps", pictures cut from books and magazines or supplied for this purpose by stationers.

ly for their veneer and genuine period base wood, and were then broken up. Sometimes linen presses were stripped, shelving was put in, and they were sold as bookcases, although they were never convincing except as decorative pieces. The dealers then realized to their chagrin that linen presses were creeping back into fashion.

Of all the antique success stories of the twentieth century, pine is one of the most interesting. After World War II it became a fashionable wood in "country cottages" and in the new styles of interior furnishing, especially in the kitchen after the plastic and polished steel nightmare. Waxed and polished, pine was the epitome of the good life. But, whatever dealers may say, it is never very old, and very little survives from before the nineteenth century. Unlike some woods, pine does not seem to age. A washing down with vinegar and water, a waxing and a polishing, and a pine dresser made 150 years ago could look as though it were made yesterday. And the dealers knew it, and made up pine dressers, often deliberately adding the rustic appeal by patching up broken sections or even, temerity indeed, replacing "broken" sections with pieces of orange boxes. They knew that they were selling an image.

What many of them did not know was that originally pine was painted or stained to imitate a more desirable wood. Some pieces,

Opposite: The "lady potters" of interwar England were Clarice Cliff, Charlotte Rhead, and Susie Cooper. Charlotte Rhead was possibly the most adventurous, but Clarice Cliff has her own inimitable niche.

Overleaf: This type of bottle, with an internal marble at the top to keep in the gas of lemonade or ginger beer, was patented by a man named Codd, and was produced unchanged from 1875 to 1930. It is still made in India.

Below: Art glass was a speciality of the French and the Americans, though the British had been supreme in "layered" glass (made in several layers of different colours). By the last quarter of the nineteenth century glass technology was at its peak; any colour could be obtained and glass could be carved, moulded, forced and contorted into every imagined shape. The art glass illustrated is fairly restrained, but of the highest quality.

especially those from Bavaria, bore painted pictures. As painted pine started to sell better than plain pine, many unscrupulous dealers began to paint pictures on their pine wardrobes and chests, then sandpaper them down to leave just the vestige of an image. The pine market became saturated, and private buyers became as interested in buying modern pine as they had been in buying period pine (it was much cheaper). A word of warning about heavy pieces of pine, such as armoires (large wardrobes). They often have no jointing and remain upright because of gravity.

CERAMICS AND GLASS

When it comes to pottery and porcelain fakes abound, and it is often difficult to know who is doing the faking. It is very easy to take out original marks and put other ones in. In genuine articles, unless they are stamped into the material, no two marks are *exactly* the same. The most valuable pieces often have no marks at all, and the seller and the buyer must judge the manufacturer for themselves, which often becomes a game of bluff and counter-bluff. Again, it must be stressed that there is nothing to equal the experience that comes from handling the genuine article and knowing as much as possible about it as possible.

Deliberate fakes of small valuables have been on the market since they were first made. Just before World War I a dealer went to

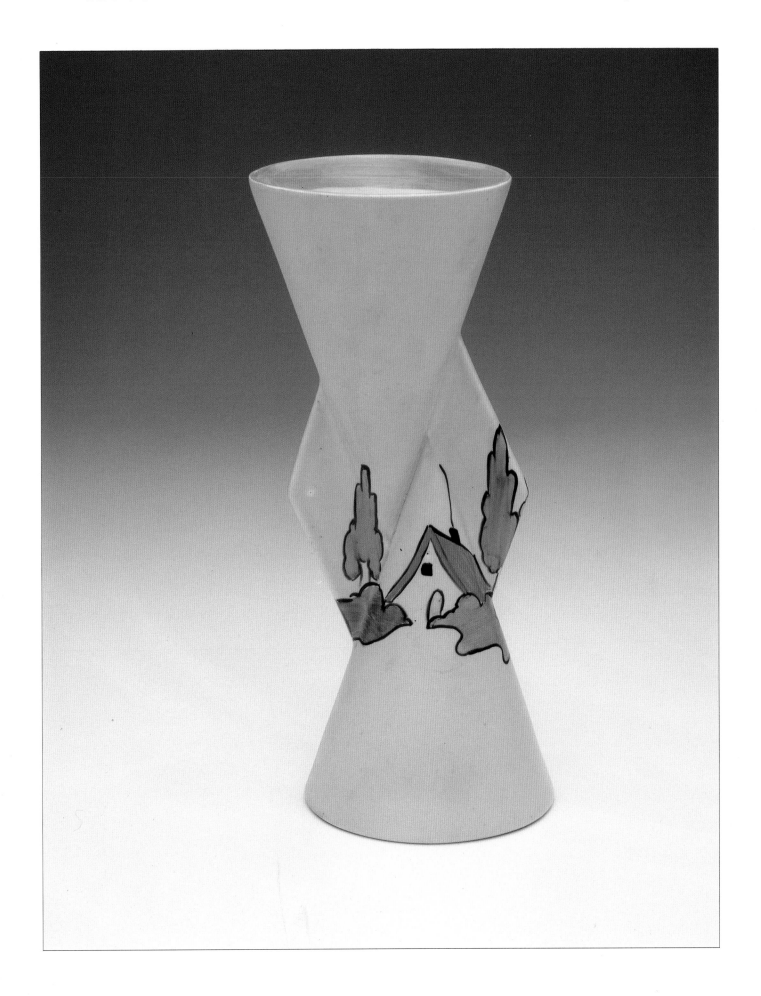

Previous page: An Art Deco figure of a boy in bronze and ivory. The most popular subjects were dancers and semi-nudes, but all were executed with amazing skill and taste; they were expensive and prestige objects for people to whom money was no object.

Opposite: A charmingly engraved glass of no great pretensions, but illustrating the ability of glass to "take" a picture. Glass engraving is highly skilled pursuit, and artists, such as Rex Whistler, are remembered through their work with glass rather than their art.

Below: Four porcelain classical figures made in Naples. The superb quality of Italian ceramics is often overlooked by writers on antiques, and the products of such factories as Capodimonte are very much subject to the whims of fashion.

Meissen, near Dresden, and looked over some old pattern books, which were even then 160 years old. He ordered a pair of figures from it. The factory was not only using the original pattern books but the original moulds. The dealer paid £70 ($108) for the figures (which was a large amount in those days), stained and scraped them, and sold them in Britain for more than £2000 ($3100) – which was some profit! Who would detect them today? And how many collectors could identify the "old" Staffordshire figures imported from Holland and France for just a few pence each? Toby jugs were another popular line with the less-than-honest. Beer would be simmered in jugs, which were then wrapped in hide and buried in the garden. They deceived the collectors ninety years ago. And today? The tricks of the trade were probably no less subtle than they are now.

Some tricks of the trade are crude. Putting a price sticker over an incipient crack can only work at markets where trade is brisk and the dealer is never seen again. A crack in a glass can be disguised by placing the glass under running water. Do not buy a glass that is dripping wet. Glass itself can be a tricky area. One of the centres of the industry was Bohemia; it is now in the Czech Republic and still produces magnificent glass.

An impressive display of jewellery nestling against a backdrop of stones and fabrics. The variety of jewellery is immense, offering scope both to collectors and specialist dealers, especially those who wish to contain their stock in a single suitcase.

CAVEAT EMPTOR

A shop with dim lighting should always be suspect. It is often deliberate, so that an unsuspecting buyer will miss damage. A prospective buyer should also be wary of something half-hidden away, as though forgotten. It could very well be a picture, and it might bear the label of a well-known picture dealer (so easily run off these days with a word processor and colour photocopier). A label of a gallery or even an old-style picture-framer is often, for some reason, more convincing than a signature, which everyone knows can be a forgery.

Sometimes old fakes are more evident now than when they were

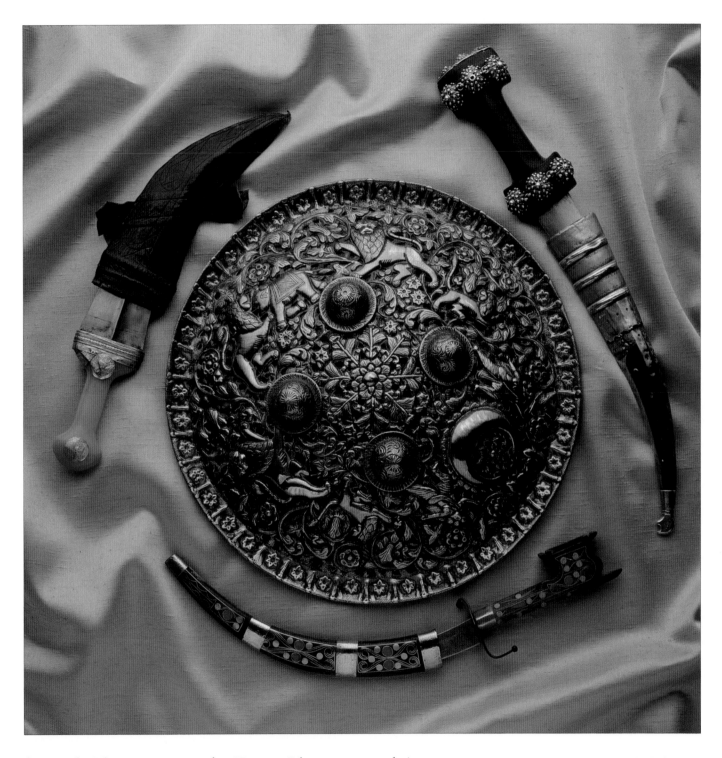

first made. There was a craze for "Benares" brass trays made in Birmingham, Warwickshire, ivories made from moulded celluloid, and "ivory" netsukes (Japanese cord holders) made from fishbones. Tsubas (Japanese sword-guards) were stamped out by machinery and sold by the gross, and Oriental bronzes have been artificially aged for centuries.

Clock movements have often been transplanted to better cases, and at one time car clocks that had a high quality movement were put into antique cases. Ordinary Victorian movements were stripped of their cases, put under glass domes and called skeleton clocks, which

Ethnic weaponry is an area in which few general dealers venture, though the variety is wide, from the make-it-yourself firearms of nineteenth-century India to the intricate tribal daggers of modern Africa, displaying craftsmanship of the highest order especially if they are ceremonial.

command much higher prices. These fakes and near-fakes are still about, and the passage of time has made them fairly convincing, even though the buying public is more knowledgeable than ever before. Unfortunately, it is not only dealers and members of the public who have become more knowledgeable. Fakers, too, have learned a thing or two. At one time crackle was put on "old" pottery too regularly, but fakers have learned discretion.

It is, however, sometimes possible to be too suspicious. What might at first glance be a fake can be a straightforward revival. The Victorians made Chippendale chairs, but altered the dimensions slightly; there was no intention to delude. Alterations have also been made to improve certain types of antiques – the bellows of pre-1895 cameras are likely to have been replaced, for instance, because they may have cracked at the folds, and some cameras were innocently modified to take different film.

Some fakes and fakers are collected in their own right. In the nineteenth century the French firm of Samson imitated almost every kind of fine china (including Chinese and Meissen porcelain) and enamelled boxes with immense care. Often their work can be detected only because of anachronistic pictorial detail. So prolific were the Samsons, that they have actually been credited with making many

Opposite: A ravishing display of tiles, mainly Victorian and art nouveau. Many famous Victorian artists such as Walter Crane and J. Moyr-Smith designed tiles, and, more important, tile pictures on and in public buildings, butchers, dairies and hospitals. Mercifully some remain intact in their original locations. Victorian wash-stands were once bought purely to get hold of the fine tiles on the splash-back.

Below: A sparkling Art Deco tureen on a tray, showing how able the maker was in contrasting different materials. Many of these supposedly functional objects were show-pieces, and did not stand up to the tough treatment of kitchen life. The enamel cracked and the angularity made washing them annoying if not difficult.

more things than they could possibly have produced.

It has been profitable (but dangerous, for in Britain it is a very serious criminal offence) to mess about with silver. It is not totally unknown for assay marks to be transferred from an unimportant piece to something desirable. Three-pronged forks, perhaps the rarest of table ware, have been made from spoons by adapting the bowl or removing the bowl and adding prongs. Teapots have been appearing on the market dated as having been made before tea was actually introduced from China. Faked silver sometimes has dirt and grime rubbed well into (genuine) hallmarks, so that an unwary buyer, busy with his magnifying glass, thinks that a genuine discovery has been made.

There are always innocent misapprehensions. Plastic imitating amber may be simply costume jewellery, which was never intended to

Above: One of the greatest names in French art glass was Emile Gallé (1846-1904), who found inspiration in Oriental glass at the Victoria and Albert Museum in London. He began exhibiting his glass, of which this is a tiny selection, in 1877. He also designed elegant fantasy furniture in the art nouveau style.

Opposite: An eighteenth-century ivory tea-caddy with tortoiseshell stringing, inlay of mother-of-pearl, and a silver panel for the family crest. As tea was expensive, the caddy was locked to stop the servants stealing it.

Horse brasses were both decorative and functional - to avert the evil eye. Most horse brasses are tourist pieces, sometimes well-rubbed to simulate age, and their popularity began in the 1930s when they were used for decorating the interiors of country cottages.

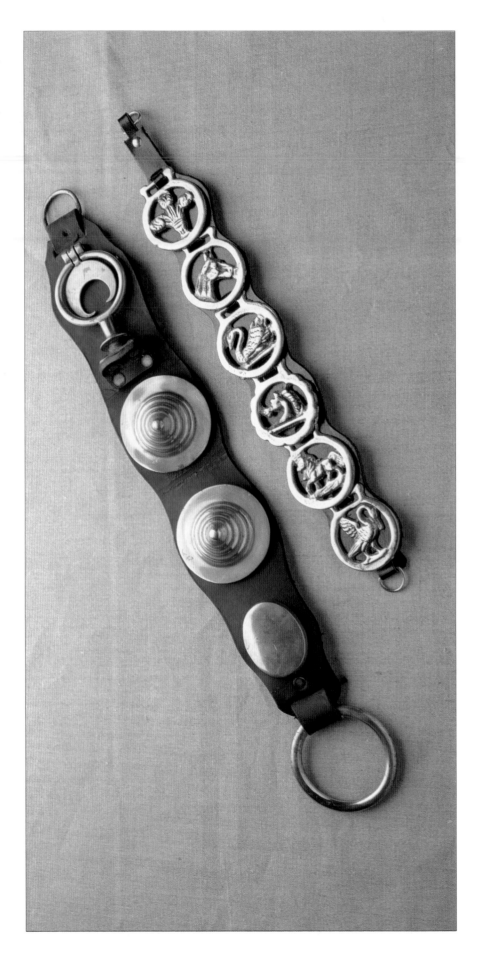

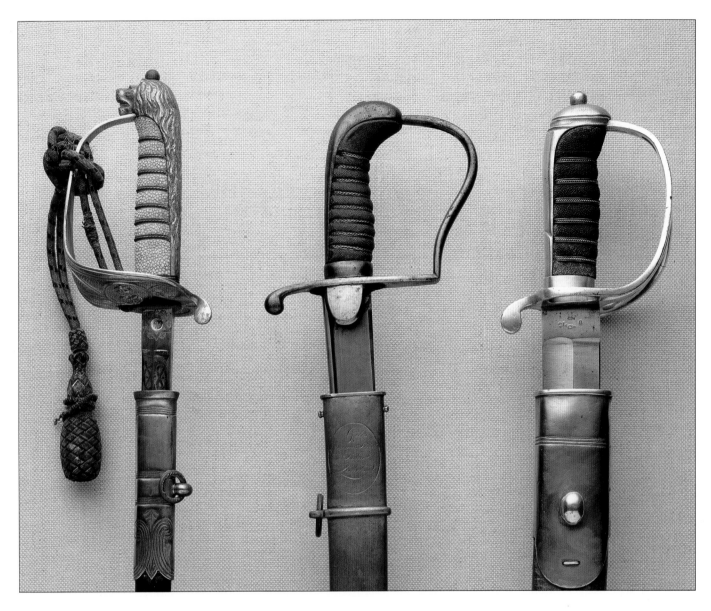

confuse. The empty glitter of "paste" is not like the lustre of a diamond, but many dealers have come unstuck – and resolved never to meddle with jewellery again.

Tricks of the trade, and tricks on the trade. The splendid blue-and-white made-yesterday Chinese porcelain in hypermarkets will soon trickle into the antique stream. The opening up of eastern Europe has brought a wealth of previously little-known types of antiques on the market. How many are fakes? Of the thousands of Russian icons, how many can be given a clean bill of health?

The hilts of British army swords; the hilts were covered with shagreen, which was either shark-skin or untanned leather. These swords were not only for ceremonial use; they were used, but to little effect, by army officers in World War I just as the British cavalrymen used lances. Neither was of much use against the machine-gun.

Buyer beware! But enjoy the quest as well.

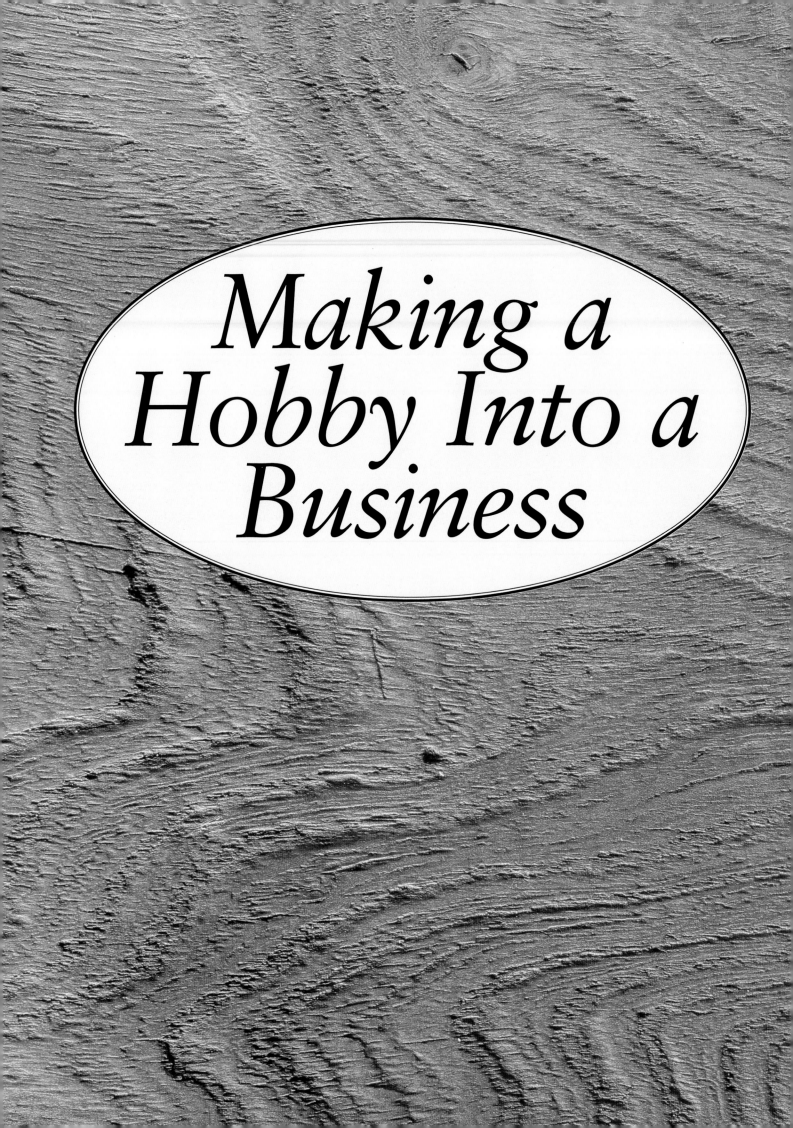

Making a Hobby Into a Business

Opposite: Two agreeable brass candlesticks. Socket candlesticks have been in existence since about 1500, but did not become fashionable until 1650. Brass was used because it was easily cleaned of candle-grease. The shape of candlesticks has not fluctuated widely since about 1700, though rather more ornate after about 1840. Reproductions are common - look for rough edges on the base. Baize-bottomed candle-sticks are suspect.

Below: The interior of a high-quality antique shop, in which nothing jars, and in which everything reflects the taste of the owner. Some antique dealers have a different philosophy - piling the stock high so that it looks as though a bargain may be found by rummaging around. It works less well than it did.

Collecting can slide imperceptibly into dealing without the collector really being aware that it is happening, for as soon as the process of discarding earlier acquisitions begins, the collector becomes a dealer, trying to obtain the best price for his collection – the essence of dealing.

Antique dealing is one of the most pleasurable of professions. Dealers have more than their share of curiosity and are always striving to learn – a dealer who does not learn soon gets left behind. They are, therefore, stimulating company even when they are also rivals, and an old stager will invariably help out a newcomer with practical advice. The percentage of rogues is probably lower than in any other comparable trade or profession.

Dealers must always be learning not only about antiques, but also about near-antiques and even about those pieces that only a decade or so ago would have been labelled "junk" and thrown away. Dealers must also be aware that everything changes, including trends, and develop a feeling about what to buy and what not to buy. At one time, for instance, fairings (imported German porcelain groups and figures bearing a motto, sometimes saucy), which had sold at fairgrounds in the late nineteenth century for sixpence or so, became enormously popular. There was great jubilation when a fairing topped £1,000 (about $1,500), a ridiculous price for a cheap novelty, and many people leapt onto the bandwagon – just as prices began to

Tin toys, especially if they have a clockwork mechanism, have escalated in value in recent years, but they are still found at modest prices. This 1908 battleship can be worth up to £8000 or $12,000. Original price? A pound or two, or a few dollars. Despite the flag, it is not American.

slide. Many established dealers had kept well away from these pieces, rightly recognizing that this was an ill-starred trend and that, because the fairings were crude, they were easy to fake. Sensible dealers kept their money for "classics" or for types of antiques that were yet to be evaluated. This is not to say that the first dealers who saw the potential of fairings were unwise or less than shrewd. But it is just as important to drop out of a trend as to drop in on it.

Antique dealing is one of the few businesses that can be started with very little capital, and the range of options is almost limitless, from becoming a general dealer to specializing in a fairly narrow field. Venturing into furniture requires considerable thought, and not simply because of prices involved. Moving and storing furniture require labour and space, and taking on staff to do the heavy work and acquiring premises bites into profits.

When there is only a limited amount of cash, a shop may be out of the question, although a surprising number of new dealers find an established trader with shop premises who is willing to share, often because a partner will contribute to the overheads such as paying telephone and electricity bills not to mention doing a stint in the shop. Running a shop always raises the problem of having to choose between keeping the shop open and going out to buy, and a partner-

A George II chest of drawers. This must be regarded as a benchmark of taste and quality, and it is salutary, when considering some lesser item of furniture, to compare it with this and see how far it falls short, in proportions, detail, fitness for purpose, and "looking right". It is far too easy to regard humdrum pieces of furniture as first rate when comparing it with much of the rubbish that is going around.

ship of some kind can be ideal in these circumstances. Often a husband-and-wife team can work well together, but it can be difficult, for no two people share exactly the same tastes – "How much did you pay for that? You must be out of your mind!"

Before dipping the toe in the real world of dealing, it might be better to start off with a flea market, a boot fair or an open market to get a taste of dealing and what is involved. If the stock is good – perhaps culled from around the house or from co-operative relatives and friends – a real antique market may be a first step. Bear in mind, however, that a stall or space can cost a lot of money – sometimes several hundred pounds or dollars – and a flea market or its equivalent will probably be less intimidating. Some markets have regular weekly venues, while some are held irregularly. All will be advertised in the local press, however. It is vital to find out if prior booking is necessary or if it is organized on a first-come-first-served basis. It is a good idea to attend such markets beforehand to see both what kind of people attend and what kind of people run the stalls.

The pleasures of dealing far outweigh the occasional disadvantages. An open market deep in mud, with rain making nonsense of carefully framed watercolours, is no fun, but many dealers do it for years – some for thirty or forty years – so that they can keep their pitch. It is

the element of the unexpected that makes antique dealing so exciting. Despite the immense amount that has been and is still being exported from Europe, there is a never-ending supply of interesting things. Many of the classic pieces have disappeared – only a limited number of the really top-class articles was made – but this does not detract from the search for the bargain. If anything, it enhances it. Good "gear" has always been expensive and in demand, and consequently it has been a game only for those with deep pockets – unless the piece is absolutely fresh from a private source. For example, a Dürer etching was bought in a street market in Devon, England, for 20p (30c) and sold later that day for £700 ($1000) without it ever leaving the area.

It is sometimes recommended that dealers should buy only what they like, but this may be unnecessarily limiting. The dealer may have an instinct for what sells or can see quality in an object that he or she does not particularly like. Quality is difficult to analyse; a quality object may not even be well made, but it will have an aura about it. Roman coins, for example, are often crude, with incompetent images of long-forgotten emperors; but they have a certain something.

Above: Lustre was imparted by applying oxides (metal) on to fired ceramics, then fired again, fixing the lustre. which could be in many colours, favourites being purple and pink. The process originated in Persia and brought to Europe via Spain.

Opposite: Sheffield plate is a substitute for silver, discovered about 1742, in which a thin film of silver was coated over a core of copper. Electroplating from about 1840 did much the same thing using electrolysis. Old Sheffield plate ages agreeably, but when the proportions of silver to copper dropped from one part in ten to one part in sixty the results could be less satisfactory.

Decoy swans are rare compared with decoy ducks. Made from wood so that they would float, they were placed on stretches of water called decoys to assure wild ducks that they were safe. The wild ducks were then shot. Decoy ducks are widely reproduced and some are faked.

These options – a shop or a stall in a market – are not the only alternatives for the aspiring dealer. Some successful dealers never have a retail outlet; they buy shrewdly and put their acquisitions into auction. Others sell from one dealer to another, taking a modest profit on each transaction. Some sell from their homes, advertising in the local papers. They do not say they are dealers, but they do not have to, for buying from and selling to whomever is not illegal. The word dealer is, in fact, a name for a lover of old things who happens to make a living at it.

If a newly fledged dealer decides to take on a shop there are certain factors to consider. Should it be in a town or in the country? If a town, should it be near the centre or on the outskirts? (A shop in the centre is often more easily found, but it will depend on the particular location. A shop in the suburbs can be a recipe for disaster.) Should it be in a village or in the middle of nowhere? The overriding question is: will the shop be visited? Fellow dealers are the target, rather than the private buyer, especially if the outlet is out of a major antique centre, such as London. If the shop is likely to be in an inner-city area, there are considerations that did not apply twenty or thirty years ago – how to protect it against vandalism, burglary and acts of wanton destruction. Defensive measures – burglar alarms, window grilles, good locks – are all very well, but a well-concealed safe is better. Small valuables should never be left in a shop.

Dealers have "runs". If they do a trip they plan it beforehand, knowing exactly where they are going, and a town with several good antique shops is always a prime target, making it worthwhile for a dealer to call, even if it means a detour off a freeway, motorway or major road. If a suitable property seems to be available, visit the town beforehand, speak to the dealers, get a feel of how they are doing. Look at price-tags to see if they are dog-eared or if the prices have been reduced. Check if objects have dust on them. Also visit unrelated shops to see if the place is prosperous. The status of the other shops will help you judge this. A plethora of cheap gift shops is bad news, for example, but some quality craft and arty shops are a decided plus. If there are no antique shops in the town or village, try to find out if there has ever been one. If there once was and it ceased trading, there was a reason – could it have been that there were no customers?

Although the existence of a number of antique shops in an area will help when it comes to visiting trade, it reduces the chance of a "call-out". This is when a "punter" comes into a shop with something to sell or wants the dealer to come to see something he or she has to sell (go with a companion, just in case). If there are several shops, the private seller will do the rounds and take the best price. A private seller is not necessarily scrupulous, and bear in mind that appearances are no guide. Many, in fact, send children in. The goods on offer may be damaged and repaired or they may be stolen, and even reputable sellers will expect cash and not a cheque. So a dealer must not only decide on the goods, but make a character assessment as well, and all on the spot. No one will wait around while the dealer dithers.

Parking facilities are another important factor. Dealers who are out on the road are not too happy about a good deal of walking. They much prefer to park in front of the shop window, whether it is permitted or not ("loading" is always the excuse for illegal parking). It is good to be on a straight road with unhampered visibility, so that a dealer has plenty of time to register the fact that there is a shop and has time to stop.

Shops may be lock-up premises, but some have accommodation above, and this can be useful because dealers will get to know that there are no strict hours – a true dealer will always open up when there is a chance of a sale. Never judge a shop on sight – a lick of paint, bright lighting and a good sign can transform a drab property. A double window is an asset, because this is your point of sale and an interesting display can bring in waverers, especially if they are private buyers. If there is storage space at the back, always keep something interesting and buyable there (even a loss leader), because dealers like nothing better than to rummage.

Good shelving is important, and deep shelves are especially valuable so that bulky objects do not fall off and break. Wooden shelving is perhaps better than glass, because the objects, being partly obscured, need closer examination. Objects on glass tend to be skipped through. Now that remote-control video cameras are relatively cheap, it is no longer quite so important to keep the shop free from blind spots, but try to disguise the camera if you have one, because high technology is

Early eighteenth-century Bristol delft charger (large plate) with oak leaf motifs. Several potteries grew up in Bristol from about 1650. The process of making delftware arrived from Delft in Holland.

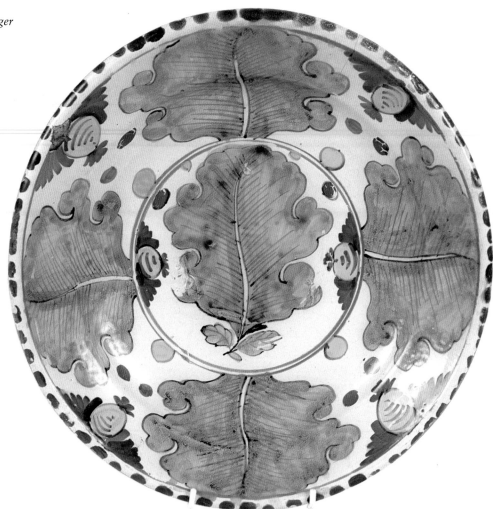

inclined to detract from the old world image.

Unlike a confectionery shop or a newsagent, an antique shop does not have a constant flow of customers, although there may be a lot of browsers. Specialist dealers can have as few as half a dozen customers in *a week*, but when they buy, they buy. If it is all too boring, paid help is a possible solution, but remember that an employee will not have the incentive to keep an eye on the stock if there are shoplifters about and may be unable to clinch a deal, not knowing how much was paid for a particular item.

Reliable transport is essential, and most dealers have a roomy estate car or something similar, usually with a roof-rack. They also develop packing goods into an art. Bubble-wrap is a boon, but crumpled-up newspaper is almost as good. When you are filling a box, pack the items in tight. Wine boxes of the kind that can be picked up from supermarkets are the best containers for "smalls", because they are not too large to carry up flights of stairs. Antique markets are often held on a first floor, especially if they are held in hotels or public halls.

Those who like open markets should equip themselves for bad weather, and a transportable polythene-covered stall is not expensive. Open markets always start earlier than the announced time – an advertised ten o'clock start actually means at least eight o'clock. In

shops and stalls there is a choice between good display and piling them high in the manner of supermarkets, even when the stock is of good quality. It often helps if a dealer casually conveys an effect of muddle and slight chaos. Who knows, thinks the buyer, what might be there?

Some shop dealers use a code on their labels rather than display a price. This is done to prevent private customers using the shop as a convenient price guide or to confuse other dealers. It has one disadvantage, however: customers are usually reluctant to ask the price in case it is too much. Few private buyers ever like say "No" outright, and they will usually say that they will think about it, not wishing to appear rude.

Shops and stalls always seem to have "selling places". For incomprehensible reasons, goods will sell from one particular spot – not necessarily the window, not necessarily the centre of the stall. Sometimes it can be under the stall. It is important to swap items around, so that they do not look stale to regular visitors. Whenever possible, keep window lighting on at night; a passer-by will often spot something and return for it the following day. An alternative is to place a telephone number on display so that a buyer can leave a message. A passer-by is always a potential buyer. And attracting buyers is the name of the game. It is as simple as that.

A pair of George III shield-back Hepplewhite chairs, upholstered in leather and not, thank goodness, in rexine. This is what antiques are about - absolute perfection. Those on a tight budget can't always find it - but they can always seek it in whatever collecting sphere they want to operate in!

Index

Picture Credits